A Gathering of Gifts

A Gathering of Gifts

Paula Lawrence Wehmiller

A
JourneyBook
from
Church Publishing Incorporated New York

Library of Congress Cataloging-in-Publication Data

Wehmiller, Paula Lawrence.
  A gathering of gifts / Paula Lawrence Wehmiller.
    p. cm.
  ISBN: 0-89869-358-6 (pbk.)
   1. Wehmiller, Paula Lawrence. 2. African American women--Biography. 3. African Americans--Biography. 4. Women educators--United States--Biography. 5. Women priests--United States--Biography. 6. Episcopal Church--Clergy--Biography. 7. Wehmiller, Paula Lawrence--Family. 8. Lawrence family. 9. Morgan family. 10. Wehmiller, Paula Lawrence--Philosphy. I. Title II. Series.
E185.97.W46 2002
305.896'073'0092--dc21
[B]

                                      2002019316

Church Publishing Incorporated
445 Fifth Avenue
New York, NY 10016

5 4 3 2 1

For John Frederick
Whose love is the strength for the journey

Author's Note

I am grateful to those who have previously published a few of the stories I tell in this book as essays, portions of chapters, journal articles and occasional papers. All of the stories have their origin in the oral tradition in which I am formed, and therefore are continually transformed by time and the mystery of becoming a part of the lives of those who hear them anew. More than a few of these stories, I have learned, have taken on a life of their own. The texts of the Negro Spirituals as I have used them to introduce each chapter are quoted as I received them, also an inheritance from the oral tradition of my ancestors. I am grateful to Frank Tedeschi and Marilyn Haskel of Church Publishing Incorporated, who heard some of these stories and urged me to gather them together between covers. It has been in the gathering that I have received the gift of hearing these stories anew myself.

Prologue

THERE IS NO WORD THAT I KNOW OF in the English language for the moment in which a story is awakened and wants telling. There is a stirring in the tree branches. There is a pounding in the chest. A passage swells in the music and suddenly there are tears. There is a moment alone in the car or on a walk, and a smile or even a laugh comes seemingly out of nowhere. It is the moment of the story's telling. I never know when it is coming, but I always know it when it has arrived. It won't be ignored. It arrives with the feelings that were stored long ago in the story's first moments of reality. The feeling has returned in this moment of the story's reawakening with a purpose that will be known only as the story unfolds.

Telling stories is the way we speak in our family. "Parable" is our mother tongue. It always surprises me when someone refers to me as a storyteller. Separating stories from who I am would be like separating breathing from the way I live my life. The stories that want telling are my way of knowing where I've come from, who I am becoming, and who I am called to be in this world. Frederick Buechner defines vocation as "the place where your deep gladness meets the world's deep need."[1] The story that is awakened and wants telling in that timeless instant is an invitation to prayer. What is God showing me in this moment of the story's telling? What gifts of discernment, naming, truth-telling, hospitality, justice, healing, forgiveness, reconciliation, celebration and love reside in the memory of the story's fabric? What wisdom does the story pass down from the ones who have gone before us? How is the story changed and shaped anew as it comes through me and is heard by fresh ears in new times and places?

---

1 In Parker Palmer, *Let Your Life Speak*, (San Francisco, CA.: Jossey-Bass, 2000) p.16

In my work as a sojourner among children, I have come to believe that children's vocation, their full-time work, is their spiritual life. And they are endowed at birth with the spiritual gifts that are the seed of that godly vocation: their capacity for paradox and parable, their ability to abandon an old idea and make room for a new one, their capacity for forgiveness, their propensity to remember, their aptitude for ambiguity, their powers of observation, their inclination toward mystery, their dreams and imagination, their vision and their faith, their unabashed longing for and seeking wholeness, their play, their prayers. Because I am blessed by a natural inclination to speak in the parables of my childhood, the prayers of my adulthood are blessedly endowed with these God-given treasures. When in the hectic way of things it ceases to be so, the children in my life see to it that I am brought back to the truth telling of my mother tongue.

Woven into the cloth of the stories gathered here are prayers of gratitude. As I pray the parables of my life, I feel God's "tender compassion…break upon me" in the generosity, support and blessing of my parents, Margaret and Charles Lawrence, and my siblings, Chuck Lawrence and Sara Lawrence. They are my fierce and loving advocates, encouraging me to live the story of who I am.

I feel God's pleasure in the love and nurturing poured out on me by our sons, John Wesley and Abram Lawrence. By living out the gifts of who they are with courage and spirit, they have, from the beginning, been my teachers and glimpses of God's promise for a better world. "They are the sons of Life's longing for itself." [2]

Henri Nouwen, in a meditation on waiting, points to the models of waiting in the first chapters of Luke's Gospel where Elizabeth and Zechariah, Mary and Elizabeth, Simeon and

---

2 Kahlil Gibran, *The Prophet*, (New York, N.Y.: Alfred A. Knopf, 1923)

Anna are representatives of a waiting Israel. He calls them "models of community" as they wait in pairs, and he adds that the community practice of waiting is not passive, but open-ended, actively waiting with expectation, knowing that what we are waiting for has already come.[3] John Wehmiller is Simeon to my Anna. He is my life partner and companion, my soul mate and friend. His love and prayers are spoken with gentleness, admiration, skepticism, laughter, tears, occasional mischief and his signature economy of expression. John's willingness to wait with me is everywhere between these lines.

Henry David Thoreau is said to have written that our friends make up the latitude and longitude of our world. The stories that those in my family of friends have told me, the ones they have listened to, and the ones we have lived together as guests in each other's homes and hearts are the ever-present answers to my prayers for direction and hope. Some of my guides reside on whatever meridians chart the Communion of Saints, so I have frequent conversations with friends who are no longer physically on this earth. I pay attention to them in dreams and listen for their voices when I am in the midst of something difficult. I feel their prayerful presence in my grandfather's ordination cross, my grandmother's hairpins, my friend Toni's amethyst ring, a Mother's Day card from Sister Lena, and my mother-in-law's gold crown ring given to her by her grandsons and now worn by me with my wedding ring to remind me that she had her very own way of praying for them and still does. I surround myself with remembrances of the four-pawed creatures whom God has sent as earthly emissaries to console me, to encourage me and, when I have been away too long, to welcome me home. I read the Daily Office from the 1979 Book of Common Prayer given to my father when, as President of the House of Deputies, he

---

3 Henri J. M. Nouwen. "A Spirituality of Waiting" (recorded lecture) (Notre Dame, IN.: Ave Maria Press, 1985)

presided over its becoming the official Prayer Book of the Episcopal Church. And I begin preaching (and praying) with the spirituals Pa sang as he held all three of his children in his lap and rocked mostly himself to sleep. These are reminders that the saints are praying for us too, "bearing us in their hands, keeping us from dashing our feet against stones"[4]; or when we do, they are here to soothe our wounds.

Prayers of invitation are gathered here too. They are prayers for you, the reader, that something in the mystery of these images and sounds, these things said and unsaid, will awaken your stories and allow you to hear the prayers God is already praying with you. I encourage you to select only what is useful to you at the moment, and save the rest for the time when that story wants telling. I wish for you a timeless time, a time of remembering, reflection, and re-imagining, a time of grace. I pray that the unfolding stories will be for you in the reading as they have been for me in the telling—*A Gathering of Gifts* from the past and seeds of nourishment for wholeness and healing.

---

4 Quote from psalm 91.

1

I got shoes, you got shoes...
All God's children got shoes.
When I get to heaven, gonna put on my shoes,
Gonna dance all over God's heaven...heaven...heaven.
Everybody talkin 'bout heaven aint goin' there!
Heaven, heaven, gonna walk all over God's heaven.

IT IS 1951, AND SUMMER HAS COME to a steady, hot, quiet hum late in August. A healthy amount of boredom in the air begins to let the summer end, making way for anticipation of my first day of kindergarten, the beginning of school. My brand new first-day-of-school dress hangs on the mirror over my bureau. Red plaid, I think, with a white collar. New cotton undies and slip and soft white ankle socks are folded on the bureau. And in an open shoe box, with white tissue paper unfolded enough to see them, are my new red school shoes. (My mother had told the salesman "something sturdy in a school shoe." I had been picturing bright red patent leather party shoes and was crestfallen when "sturdy" signaled the salesman to bring out brown shoes with a tie.) Mom and I must have persevered, each with her own image of what my first school shoes would be, because I ended up with oxblood red leather with a double strap and double buckles — pretty but sturdy — "handsome" was my father's peacemaking word for the compromise shoes. Every end of August night before going to bed, I would carefully lift the shoes out of the crisp paper, smell the fresh, new leather, put them on the floor next to my feet and think, "I am going to school. I'm going to step up the big high steps onto scary Mr. Gurky's scary big school bus where

. . . . . .

I've heard the big kids chant, "Kindergarten baby, stick your head in gravy" when the little kids get on. I'm going to real school in a strange new place. *Will anybody know who I am?*

✳ ✳ ✳

It is thirty-seven years later. I am sitting in my room at the school where I have just begun my second year as principal. The principal's office has been painted a calming adobe white, and I have filled it with familiar treasures — paintings, pottery, weavings — gifts from children I have taught. A photograph of my parents standing arm in arm in front of our home beams out over my shoulder. An Easter-morning image of my husband and two sons walking along the beach, the sunrise at their broad shoulders, reassures me. And my sturdy rocking chair welcomes the littlest visitor to a cozy lap or offers my own back solid support when a tougher customer comes around. I have tried to make my room an oasis in the hectic world of school.

It is late August and, as I sit in my room working on scheduling and carpools, signing requisition forms and answering anxious phone calls, I have a sense of a great August tide coming in from the outside world. All that late-summer boredom washing over the families, all those shopping trips for new school clothes, all that talk in the aisles of the grocery store or the parking lot of the mall about which teacher your child got and whether her best friend is in her class. All that anticipation. And right then, as I glance out of my window to the front yard of the school, comes someone who couldn't wait for the first day. It is four-year-old Libby Sailor, bright round face, big brown eyes, shiny clean hair, brand new crisply ironed red plaid cotton dress with big white collar, and handsome red school shoes. She has climbed out of the car and is walking bravely toward the school. Her mother, somewhat less bravely, is trying to catch up from many steps behind. Libby has come to school with a wondering in her heart: *Will anybody know who I am?*

The sojourner stands at the door holding a gift in her hands. It is the gift of her story, her experiences, her dreams. It is the gift of her longing and hopefulness, her relationships with her family and friends. She holds the gift even of her hurting and wanting and doubts. She holds the gift of her questions, even the ones she does not yet know to ask. She holds the gift of her thirst for life. *Will anybody know who I am?* Will anyone know what I can do? Will anyone see what gift I hold in my hands?

The question is at once a child's question and a prophet's question. It is one that is asked as we step onto Holy Ground. It is a question that speaks of a longing to be known. It is an invitation to discover the newcomer's Unseen Self, to discover the spiritual gifts that are revealed when the community gathers to hear the story's telling. And it is an invitation to remember our own stories too. *Will anyone know who I am?*

It is late in August of 1963, a sweltering, hot summer day between high school graduation and my first year of college. The old, rickety school bus painted over light blue and lettered with the name of a Baptist church has brought me safely to this spot where I kneel on the grass beside the reflecting pool in the shadow of the Lincoln Memorial, my hand unconsciously moving the still, dark, healing water through my fingers. I am at once alone and a part of something much bigger than this moment in time can gather. Two hundred and fifty thousand people have put on their shoes and journeyed here by train and bus, by plane, in cars, some on foot from the D.C. neighborhoods, none of us knowing or even imagining, I suspect, what moment we will look back on thirty years later.

My seventeen-year-old heart is filled with fear as I climb the steps of this bus full of strangers in the cooler early morning hours back in Nyack, New York. It is not unlike the cool mornings of my childhood years, dutifully climbing the big yellow school bus steps because I knew I must, even as I would quickly learn that the daily journey would separate me by more than the country roads we traveled from the sanctuary of home. I am thankful at this moment for the years of practice climbing these steps against my will, because I know I must take this trip now.

The press has punctuated the headlines and airwaves with frightening rumors of possible rioting and mass arrests in Washington. "Stay home," they warn us. But right now a more urgent voice is lifted up into my heart. It is the voice of a lifetime of stories told round the family table, on family trips, and in the holy moments of my parents sitting on the edge of my bed in the safe darkness of my room having tucked me between the crisp, clean sheets for the night. I hear their patient, careful answers to my frightened questions about lynchings and bus-burnings in the South. "Could they come here?" I remember asking when my mother found me weeping in my sleep in the middle of the night. I'd been dreaming of our two-room school house where my brother and sister and I were the only brown-skinned children—the buttoned-down desks and slate blackboards all blown up in splinters and flames. And though I cannot remember my parents' words, I feel the comforting tones of their voices and the warmth of my mother's hand in my hand, my father's big hand squeezing my shoulder as they bravely, simply taught their children through and beyond the anger and pain of their own firsthand memories of indignities done to our people. And then as if my feet have their own memory of what my parents taught us next, I am lifted up the steps of this bus bound for the March on Washington. Something in me and beyond me is carrying on.

✳ ✳ ✳

Now as the driver pulls closed the large, silver lever of the folding door, as the old bus coughs and sputters away from the curb, I find myself comforted by the press of my seatmate's large right arm against my left shoulder, my right shoulder against the now foggy bus window, also familiar from years of crowded school bus rides. We are not all the way down the block before the bus is filled with singing, and the pounding of fear in my chest makes itself at one with the heartbeat of the song rising up to fill the air: *"I got shoes, you got shoes, all God's children got shoes."* My voice easily finds the harmony it has found all my life at the family table, on long car rides away, on shorter car rides back home, in church, and as we picketed on the sidewalk outside the local Woolworth's. As the chorus grows stronger, I am feeling the presence of those who had the courage long before us to put some battered shoes on their weary feet and march away from the enslavement of those who would never know the gift of who they were inside. *"Everybody talkin' 'bout heaven ain't going there!"* The familiar songs and my voice's place in them connect me now to my story, the family story, the story the family tells about my people's story, the gift of who I am. The singing itself transforms fear into courage and brings me home to myself.

Two hours later, as I step down off the bus in the now hot, crowded city, my body is moved into the march with the others. It is a march I've been on as long as I can remember and I feel no crush in the crowd—only a oneness with a people who know how to bring strength out of struggle, people marching home to ourselves.

We are gathered, now in that oneness, a carpet of colorful humanity, shoulder to shoulder, singing, listening to speeches, some shouting back, all of us joined by our common struggle to manage our hot, sweaty, thirsty selves and our aching feet.

I sit on the grass beside the reflecting pool, my right hand gently sweeping through the cool, calming water. Then in a moment I cannot recollect the beginning of but will never forget being in the midst of, Martin Luther King, Jr. speaks these words into a thundering silence: *"I have a dream that my four children will one day live in a nation where they will not be judged by the color of their skin but by the content of their character."*

· · · · · ·

In this moment by the healing waters of the reflecting pool, I know that Martin Luther King, Jr. sees me, sees us, as a people. He is not seeing us by the color of our skin or the circumstances of our lives, but by the gathered gifts in which we live and move and have our being. As Dr. King speaks of his dream, the nightmarish demons of institutionalized racism give way to a new dream in me. His words become forever the words to my story, our story, and in the cool waters of that healing moment, the fever of the sweltering day dissipates into the humid summer air. I turn in this healing moment of my heart's gladness toward a lifetime's vocation: seeking to open doors so that every child is free to come in, to come home to the self that is God's gift to each of us.

Late on a September evening in 1963, I am sitting on the edge of the bed in the room of my childhood, anticipating yet another first day of school. I am packing my suitcase and getting ready to leave home to go to college. My father has counseled me to spread my more-than-plentiful gear out into two or three small bags so that I can handle them more easily. But I persevere with the stubbornness I was born with, packing it all into one gigantic, heavy suitcase.

I have gone to Junior Whirl, the up-to-date dress shop in our tiny town, to pick out my college clothes. Into my suitcase I carefully fold the white, bulky-knit collegiate sweater that I selected; a black-watch plaid, box-pleated skirt with a vest to match; and a crisp white blouse with a peter-pan collar. Against my inclination to take only pretty things, I pack the sensible, oxblood red leather English walking shoes my mother had urged me to buy. Even as I pack them, I know I will never wear them once I get to school. I also tuck in a pair of Capezio dancing shoes which I will eventually wear every day for four years, until they have little on the bottom and hold on to my feet by their pretty little straps only because I love them so.

Along with the carefully folded clothes, I pack in that suitcase my music and art and dance, my love of sports, my imagination, my stories, my humor, my dreams. I am certain to pack my optimism, my toughness and stubbornness, my strictness and high expectations of myself, my visions of all it is possible to do and be. I pack, too, the resounding notes of my parents' frequent refrain to all their children: You know who you are, and you are blessed.

Off I go to Swarthmore College with my one, big suitcase banging unevenly along on one side of me, just as my father had said it would. When I arrive at the campus, I look up the broad walkway to the forbidding, staunch, gray building with its heavy, narrow doors, and I say to myself, "I will never dance and dream and sing and laugh in this scary place. And surely, this is no place to tell my stories. I will never even be able to get this suitcase through the door! I'd better leave this suitcase right here."

And so I carefully tuck my dream away and with it the truth about who I am. College needs me to be somebody else—someone who can do the important things, the serious things, and do them well: kingdom, phylum, class, order, family, genus, species, SATs, GREs, MCATs and LSATs, prepare for graduate school, prepare for a job, boot camp for life! For four years I keep my dream a secret against every intuitive bone in my body, but then I know too well how to do that—a lifetime of practice going through the doors of schools where the story they were telling was not our family's story, did not connect me to our people's story.

There the bag sits at the bottom of the long, broad walkway while I plow through four years of lectures, labs, papers and exams, choices, decisions, successes and failures. Now and again, I peek out of the dormitory window to see my big, old suitcase covered with snow or leaves or soaked with the rain, patiently waiting for me to be done fitting in the best I can. All the while, I am wondering, "Without the contents of my suitcase, will anybody know who I am?" On the day of graduation, June twelfth, 1967, I pick up my Swarthmore College diploma and my big, old, now-worn suitcase, and head for New York City.

✳ ✳ ✳

It is late in August of 1969, and I am standing in the doorway of the school room where, in a few weeks, I will begin my career as a teacher. A strong ray of late-afternoon sun makes its way down the narrow cobblestone alley and through the classroom window, forming a circle of light on the floor where a circle of six-year-olds soon will gather. Here at last, I am thinking, I can unpack that big old suitcase. In this place, I will be able to tell my stories and sing my songs. The room invites my colors and my imagination. Here, the dream will be allowed to live again.

The dream would live again because the children who soon came through that door demanded to know the truth about who I was. They challenged me to tell my story and insisted that they be allowed to become part of that story too. The dream was their dream— to be known by the content of their character, to not have to unforget who they really were inside. They stretched me to unpack all that I had in my suitcase, including my stubbornness, my toughness, my high standards, and especially my optimism. As a teacher I could give my gifts. I could be myself. I could say for myself and with fierce optimism for those who would come through the door, *They will know who we are by the gathering of our gifts.*

2

Hush, Hush, Somebody's calling my name.
Hush, Hush, Somebody's calling my name.
Hush, Hush, Somebody's calling my name.
Oh my Lord, Oh my Lord,
What shall I do? What shall I do?

I AM LYING ON MY BACK. Maybe I am in a crib or a baby carriage, but I am not on someone's lap. I am alone but I am not lonely. My eyes are following the yellow-green sparkles of light through a hazy screen. My arms are free and my hands reach to touch what my eyes can see and my heart can feel. I feel breath in me and in the trees and gently whirling between us.

Forty-five years later I ask my mother whether our house in Nashville, where I was born, had a porch. At first she says she can't remember. I am thinking, How can she forget a house we lived in? "Tree tops," I say, "where I might have been taking a nap in a baby carriage, looking through the screen at tree tops." Still she remembers nothing. She goes over some other houses from early on, but they have no porches. Then I remember the sound of traffic going by. "Was there a street?" I press on. It feels important to me to remember. "A street. Yes, there was Meharry Boulevard. We lived in Mr. Price's house, and oh, how he loved you. He'd come up the back steps and—oh yes, you were napping on the side porch." But Mom is so anxious to tell me the rest that she doesn't pause on the answer to my original question. "Mr. Price would bound up the porch steps, lift you up in the air and bellow out, 'I love my little Charlie!'"

Yes. This is what I remember. Not Mr. Price. Not a person. But the feeling. I remember the feeling of being at peace, the feeling of the breath of God at once hidden deep within me and all around me, the feeling of being expectant, of being lifted up, of being safe and loved and adored in everlasting arms. It is a treasure that God hides inside of me and then sends me on a lifetime of seeking to find it. One day I will hear a call that draws me back to the place of this hidden treasure. And as it is revealed to me, I will hear the rejoicing: Somebody's calling my name.

The rooms in our house in Corona, Queens, are small and attached to each other without hallways. I am two years old, and I share a tiny room off of the crowded kitchen with my sister—double-decker beds, I think. I am on the bottom bed. I love this room in the daylight hours that are filled with our sisterly conspiracies. Though there are few toys, we make up stories and plays. There is lots of laughter and fun in the daylight. But I don't like the dark in this room at night, and I count on the soft, yellow light coming from the kitchen into our room. It takes away the shadows. I also count on the voices, my parents' voices. They talk to each other when we are in bed at night and though I hear only tones and rhythms, I find the talk soothing.

My brother's room is far away in the basement where we often play in the daytime. There are blocks down here and our same-size children's chairs. Chuckie and Sara and I play family. I don't know what Sara and I are in the family, but Chuckie is the father. He gives big bear hugs like the real father. There is funny old laundry equipment in the basement corner next to a little bathroom. Mom is seeing to the laundry and we talk. Or maybe I just watch. This little dark, damp corner of the basement feels safe.

My brother shares the sleeping part of the basement with our uncle. I don't question why he lives with us or why he shares a room with my brother. I don't recall his coming or going. I only know that his mouth smiles tenderly, his voice is comforting, and though his eyes are quick to tears, it is from my uncle that I learn early on to accept and even welcome the presence of tears as a gift. It is also because of the way he loves all of us unconditionally that I come to think of his living with us as evidence of angels—beautiful, brown angels.

The back door opens onto wooden steps and a patch of yard. A big old peach tree fills what little bit of yard there is. In the summer time, the peaches are so big that my father has to cut them in half for us. Not even my brother can finish a whole one. I can smell the peaches from my room in the summer time. I can't remember a window, but I can smell the peachy air as I lie in my bed. Neither my hands nor my eyes can reach for these tree branches, but my heart can feel what is in the air.

I am lying on my back between the clean, cold sheets of my bottom-decker bed. Only the hint of the springs of my sister's top-deck show in the little bit of yellow light from the kitchen. The house is quiet. "Sara," I begin and then wait in the silence for her answer which I know will come, as it is a part of an ongoing life conversation between sisters. "Do you know the Holy Ghost?" "No," she answers quietly. "Do you?" "No," I say.

My grandparents have lived with us from the time I was born, but they must have stayed back in Corona for a while, because it is only the five of us who live in two tents in the woods the summer of clearing the land for our new house in the Hudson Highlands. One tent is for the three children and one tent for my parents, both are big army surplus canvas hung over wooden platforms. We are frequently warned not to touch the canvas from the inside when it rains or the water will drip through. For me, trying it is irresistible, and I always end up with a wet sleeping bag for a long, wet night. I love when it rains at night, and still the sound of rain on the roof of a tent is one that can help me settle into sleep just by imagining it.

We have a real icebox in the clearing set aside for a "kitchen," and a food shelf that my parents have pounded into a tree to keep the wildlife from feeding on our breakfast. Sara and Chuckie and I go to town with my dad to buy a big, clear, fresh block of ice. I don't remember the iceman's name, but I can still hear the way my father speaks to him—and everyone else we meet. If Dad forgets someone's name for the moment, he draws himself up to his full height, reaches out his hand, looks into the person's eyes and says, "Forgive me, I've forgotten your name for the moment." By this time, the person is so honored by his greeting, no one minds that he's temporarily forgotten their name. I love to go on errands with my father and have some of that honored and honoring presence rub off on me.

That summer, when the woods are finally cleared and the foundation laid for our new house, my mother and I stand in what will become my room with my brother's and sister's rooms on either side. Mom says that she and Dad have decided that Sara and Chuck will have doors to the hallway. My framed-glass door will be to the outside. (I can get to the hallway through my sister's room when we aren't fighting about something, which is surprisingly little of the time.) My room, my own little sanctuary where I can lie on my back and let my eyes follow the yellow-green sparkles of light through the glass. My parents knew somehow what would be just right for me: a room set apart, open to the tree branches where I can reach to touch what my eyes can see and my heart can feel—in me and in the trees, gently whirling between us. My home inside my home where somebody's calling my name.

· · · · · ·

***

It is Sunday and the St. Paul's Episcopal Church bell is ringing. We inch around in the crowded aisle to find our places. Miss Mary McLeod is straightening our little red hats, pulling and tugging at the cottas our grandmother has starched and ironed to a fare-thee-well, and giving us little ones ungentle shoves to our places in line at the front, behind the crucifer. I hear the priest's voice droning on in competition with the uneven ringing of the bell. "Deliver us, when we draw nigh to thee, from coldness of heart and wanderings of mind," he is saying.

I know that means me, whose "wanderings" are being called in. In from my solitary play as I cross the little brook where I discovered the magic of putting a green leaf under the water and turning it into silver. In from crossing the big brook that leads to the pond where first I learned to put my head all the way under and then miraculously could swim. In from collecting blackberries, some for eating and some for pies. In from creating fantastic hairdos with my best friend, Gretchen. In from walking through the woods where she and I name the rocks and the trees and the clouds and where we are safe to name our secret fears. In from the path to Mrs. Clarke's house, where my sister and brother make me walk ahead of them because they're afraid of her fierce, little, barky dog Farmer and I'm not. In from skipping down the Wolfes' hill where my sister and I laugh ourselves silly giving each other out-of-control rides in outgrown baby-doll carriages, where we careen into the poison ivy which she gets and I don't. In from the stretch in front of the Bakers' house where my brother lopes and flows down the road, tossing imaginary fly balls into the air, catching them in his beloved mitt, turning and faking a throw to put the guy out at third. In from "Plot #33," the community ball field, where I am confident in my batting and catching but not my throwing, and where time spent playing ball is far outweighed by time spent arguing life's lessons in justice and peace. In from the top of the Iversens' hill where I hear the clear tones of my father's trumpet playing "I dream of Jeannie with the light brown hair." The church bell's uneven ringing summons us in from our wanderings, and I hear my father's trumpet summoning me home with a song that calls my name.

My father says that we have attended Sunday school so long that the little attendance pins are soon going to be down to our knees. I have made no secret of not liking Sunday school, and though I am not old enough to be a choir member, I wage a campaign to get out of Sunday school to sing in the choir instead. Even without me, the Lawrence family makes up half the choir, and I feel triumphant when the choir director makes an exception to the rule and lets me join.

Now the organist is pumping out her introduction, the last bars of "Faith of our fathers, holy faith! We will be true to thee til death." My voice soon finds its place on the alto line, and my feet find their place in this ancient and ongoing line of worshipers. As we move up the aisle, the familiar voices from the congregation are added to ours, and we are all more or less gathered in from our coldness of heart and wanderings of mind, like the priest said.

Wanderings of mind never really cease for me. My eyes and mind are drawn past the promise of being allowed to be in the parade of red robes and white cottas. Indeed, my heart longs with great jealousy for what the boys get to do in church. Mystery and beauty and rhythm and dance I see in their moves. They are bearing torches, lifting the cross, carrying this, dipping for that, bowing and scraping. Surely they are doing the Lord's work! And why are there no women preaching, absolving, blessing, reading the lessons, saying the prayers, serving bread and wine? There aren't even women on the vestry, though in my child's eye view, that just means that my mother will not be out on Monday nights. And because my mother is a physician, I think of women as natural healers. Why aren't there women doing that in church? Worst of all is staying behind while the solemn parade of people files up the steps and through the rood screen to take Communion. I feel a tinge of hunger and more than a bit of sadness as I watch the people go by to be fed. I feel sadder still that a woman is not allowed to feed them.

Because I am the youngest of the three Lawrence children, by the time I am eleven I have seen the confirmation ritual two years in a row. I can't wait! Thursday afternoons after school, I walk alone up the hill on South Main Street and turn left on Madison toward the church. For years I've watched with envy while the St. Joe's kids get to cut Wednesday mornings at school for "relig" classes. And of course the Temple Bethel kids get to go to Hebrew school, though they don't get to miss real school for that. They have to go after, when school is out.

Now it is my turn to do the mysterious thing and I feel proud. I am, it turns out, prouder than I am interested. Reverend Zeltner is a sweet and decent human being. (What more can you ask of a priest?) But as an adolescent, I think of him as an old, boring man. He gives us little blue booklets to memorize. *"What dost thou chiefly learn in these Articles of thy Belief?"* this tiny tome asks me, and I dutifully memorize the answer: *"First, I learn to believe in God the Father, who hath made me, and all the world."* At the moment, it seems unrelated to anything I feel, much less believe. But I am good at memorizing things I don't understand. I practice that lesson in school every day. All I know is that this is going to get me through that rood screen with everyone else. I am going to be allowed to join the feast.

$$***$$

On June ninth, 1957, I stand in my white confirmation dress on the front porch of the house next to my godmother, Dr. Jean A. Luke. I have heard the story of my godmother for whom

I am named Paula Jean, and it is this parable that I rehearse in my mind as I stand proudly next to my namesake.

In 1932, my mother, Dr. Margaret Morgan Lawrence, was one of the first Negro students admitted to the college of Arts and Sciences at Cornell University. Since the dormitories were still segregated at the time, my mother lived in the attic of a white family's house, and served as their maid, taking her meals from kitchen leftovers when everyone else was done eating. After graduation, she attended Columbia medical school (Cornell medical school had rejected her because another Negro had once upon a time applied and ended up getting tuberculosis, so they said that it just wouldn't work out.) At Columbia, the dormitories for medical students were for men only, and housing for nurses was segregated. So again my mother lived off campus, this time with a wealthy, white woman medical student who at age forty had conquered all but the physical effects of childhood polio and could not climb the nurses' dormitory stairs. These two, who had become roommates as a result of exclusion, became lifelong friends and leaders in their field, two women against all odds in a movement that would one day follow and eventually honor them.

At church, when it is my turn, I kneel at the crossing on the dark red velvet cushion in front of Bishop Charles F. Boynton. I feel his strong hands solidly on my head. In his warm, deep voice he is saying, *"Defend, O Lord, this thy child with thy heavenly grace."* By this time the bishop has moved on to my confirmation partner, but I still feel the weight of his hands on my head. *"This thy child with thy heavenly grace."* As the words echo in my heart, I feel something move high in my chest. This is about me. This is about Paula Jean going to the feast.

Back at home, Godmother Jean gives me a leather-bound Bible with my name on it: *Paula Jean Lawrence*—fully a person, allowed to come to the Lord's table and be fed. One day I will read the psalms to people who long to be fed by the comfort they sing. I will read to them from Aunt Jean's Bible. And when I do, the smell of the leather will bring back the "heavenly grace" of something moving in my chest. Somebody's calling my name.

"Paula Jean," my father calls out from the living room where he is seated in front of a mid-afternoon roaring fire. It is Sunday, and the great feasts of the day are over. The fragrance of Sunday dinner, lingering in the air, mixes with the smell of newly lit kindling, presence still of the love of the feasts themselves. The presider, the celebrant, having restored our three-generation household of church-goers with ample food for body, soul and spirit, has built a fire with wood freshly split with his ax. *"Roll, Jordan, roll."* His voice reaches the house from the edge of the woods as his right hand slides along the handle toward the blade end, the ax swinging through the sky in an ark and down toward the log, splitting the log in time to Papa's song.

Now he seats himself in his big, red chair, folds his Sunday *Times* "for perusal," he says, and for the first time on the Sabbath, he allows himself a full-blown sigh. I hear his settling-in sounds from my place at the kitchen sink where I am taking my turn washing the considerable dishes, evidence of Pa's generous meal preparations. I know the next sound will be the sound of my baptismal name.

"Paula Jean," he calls, and that is all he has to say. I know that he is thirsty. And so without another word from him or me, I put down my dishwater things, pick up the clay pitcher, and head out the front door and across the drive to the overflow of the artesian well. I know which rocks at the overflow's edge can be counted on for steadying myself as I bend down and dip the pitcher into the circle of still, dark water.

Now I am down on my belly on the cool, damp ground, reaching through the fragrant watercress that leans with me over the clear, dark pool. I pause on the reflection of the water-gatherer. I am surprised to see the Paula Jean who peers at me through the still-unrippled water. Her eyes, peaceful, playful and full of life, look back at me and invite me to take a drink of my own. And so I put the pitcher down in the clumps of watercress at the edge of the overflow; and cupping my hands, I bring the cool, fresh water to my mouth. I hadn't known until this moment that I was thirsty. On my way back inside, I hear in my head the tune of another of Papa's songs: *"I've just come from the fountain, I'm just from the fountain, Lord. Just come from the fountain, His Name so sweet!"*

It is Sunday evening, and by now we are all drawn to the living room by the crackling sounds and smell of my Papa's roaring fire. I sit on the floor by the hearth, my face fully turned to the heat. Our dog, Sky, has been called in for the night, and, after several turns in place, he settles down beside me, his healthy, wet nose nuzzled under the hand he knows I hold ready for him in my lap. Behind me I know by heart the settling down sounds of this evening ritual. My mother has spent her days putting her physician hands to healing hurting children and their parents in hospitals and schools. She has spent her days and nights putting her mothering and daughtering hands to healing her own children and her own parents at home. And now her hands find their way to the piano where the spirituals that roll gently out into the evening air are healing in themselves.

"There is a balm in Gilead," she begins, *"to make the wounded whole."* My father's voice is lifted on the melody. Now my sister joins in on the descant and my brother on a sweetly rolling bass. And now, the alto that has been singing silently inside of me since before the song began, finds a place for its voice and we are singing in full harmony. *"Sometimes I feel discouraged and think my work's in vain. But then the Holy Spirit revives my soul again."* As we come to the last verse my father gets up to stir the fire. The songs of weariness and weeping drowned in hope, the family-sung parables of victory over slavery and oppression and

turning toward freedom's new name, are stored in the sounds and images of my Papa's fire, forever burning signs of God's presence and love, unconditional and unconsumed.

✳ ✳ ✳

On June twenty-seventh, 1998, I sit at the prayer desk in the choir of the Cathedral Church of the Saviour in Philadelphia, freshly clothed in a flowing red chasuble. I have just been ordained a priest in the Episcopal Church. It is a hot day and a rainbow of ribbons adorning my new vestments flutters in the breeze of the electric fans. In spite of the air's movement, there is a stillness, a presence I feel but don't try to capture. I feel at peace.

My sister deacon is setting God's table. My brother priest is, as my grandmother would say, "seeing to things" as he always does. They have told me in the vulnerable days of preparation leading up to this day that they will take care of everything. All I need to do is "receive." So I wait. I wait to receive.

My father's death came long before this day. But his understanding that I was a priest came long before that. He knew before I did, and trusted me, as he did with all things, to discover it for myself. He was always willing to wait.

And now here in the waiting is the sound of the trumpet playing the offertory. *"There is a balm in Gilead to make the wounded whole."* Or is it my father's trumpet calling me in from my wanderings, calling for the treasure that God hid inside of me before I was born and then sent me on a lifetime of seeking to find it? The trumpet's clear tones call me back to the place of this hidden treasure and I hear the rejoicing: Somebody's calling my name.

. . . . . .

3

Oh Mary, don't you weep, don't you moan.
Oh Mary, don't you weep, don't you moan.
'Cause Pharaoh's army got drownded.
Oh, Mary, don't you weep.

IN THE TRIBES OF OUR AFRICAN ANCESTORS, it was the sacred duty of the elders to remember the tribal history, and so we were blessed by the presence of three generations in our growing-up household. Grandmother, Mrs. Mary Elizabeth Smith Morgan, had raised my mother in Mississippi. Her husband, the Rev. Mr. S. A. Morgan, was an Episcopal priest, and wherever he went to start a new parish, Mrs. Morgan started a school. She believed that there was no such thing as a child who could not learn, and she acted with fierce passion on that belief. She literally found lost children and mined for their strengths. It was up to her, she felt, to figure out how to teach that person in a way that she could, as she said, "get her lessons."

By the time I knew my grandmother, she had officially retired from her years of sojourning as a teacher. But she had plenty of teacher in her left to last for us. When our grandparents came to live with us soon after I was born, Grandmother took it upon herself to teach her daughter's three children the important lessons of life.

We had walked a mile down the long hill from the bus stop after school. As we came in the house each of us called out the expected greeting, "Good afternoon, Grandmother and Grandfather." And from the back of the house came the call, "OOooo! Is that you, Pauloo?" I knew that as soon as I had made a run for the bathroom and back out to the kitchen to the refrigerator to make a folded over bread-and-butter sandwich, which I actually made

· · · · · ·

standing in the open door of the refrigerator in case I wanted another one right quick, I knew that Grandmother would ask, "Did you get your lessons today?" I was always glad when I had. She was far too willing to take up the challenge.

Grandmother was tough and she was sweet. Everyone outside of the family was treated to her sweet side. The way she held her skirt with one hand and held the other so that just the right index finger was gently poised on her ample bosom; the way she held her teacup with her pinky out and insisted that we do the same; and the way she "tipped" when she had to excuse herself in company and especially from church, one hand hiking the skirt to the knee, the other hand held high with the index finger extended toward the heavens to hold her place in time.

But in the family we knew her tough side. She had rules: a bath every day at 4:30 except on Wednesday, and she'd park a brush on the side of the tub to remind us we were in there for serious bathing and not for fooling around. Sometimes if my sister and I bathed together, we'd push the limits enough for Grandmother to come to the door and lift the brush up silently. As soon as she shut the door, we'd burst into imploding fart-bubble giggles. I never let myself think what she might have done with that brush. "Set the table after bath while your hands are still clean," and "better set an extra place in case your mother brings company." A lot of her rules were about the way we spoke and especially about the way we spoke to her. "No thank you," in answer to a question was followed by, "No thank you, Grandmother." You had to say the whole thing.

The toughest thing I ever knew about Grandmother was that when my mother was a little girl, Grandmother killed chickens for supper by going out to the side of the house and ringing their necks with her bare hands. I think because I had the fairest skin of her three grandchildren, and because she had lost her first child, an infant with fair skin, she let me have her sweet side most of the time. But since I knew about those chickens, her tough side served its purpose just as well.

Grandmother was tough, but she wasn't scary. In my lifetime, she did only one thing that I found downright frightening: She tried to learn how to drive a car. When a stop light came into view, no matter how far up ahead it was, Grandmother would slam on the breaks and stop right there. On the other hand, if the brake lights of the car ahead of her lit up, that didn't phase Grandmother in the least. She would just keep sailing toward them until my father ordered her to stop. Grandmother never passed her driver's test. I still think my father might have had a little talk with the officials down at Motor Vehicles.

I liked to watch my grandmother's hands. She could bake a cake from scratch with the touch of an angel. She could snap beans with a rhythm that would put me in a trance. And though she cooked the life out of vegetables, I liked when it was greens she was cooking. She'd save a little pot liquor, and we'd each have some from the same "squatty" cup. I imagined that the dark, hot, brown-green liquid was a strength potion. Maybe it was. As an adult when I drink from the cup at Communion I still taste that pot liquor.

By day, I attended school where they taught us about "the War Between the States," (or "That Late Unpleasantry," as my junior high school social studies teacher called it. She was still protecting the sale of textbooks in the South). But by night, school took place as I sat on the children's chair between my grandmother's knees and learned the Family Parable of the Emancipation Proclamation during our nightly hair-brushing sessions. Grandmother would tell me to go get the brush and comb and have me pull one of the children's chairs up between her knees, and she would go at my hair with the same fierce passion with which she approached the knotty problems of her teaching days. One hundred strokes minimum, and when she got to the "kitchen"—that tender and tangled place that every Black child of God knows at the nape of the neck—there was no mercy. The more tangled it was, the more she was satisfied to go in there and get those knots. I learned early on that if I held very still and gave her a little resistance, I was better off.

Much of Grandmother's life was a mystery to me. When I asked her questions about her growing-up life, she frequently told me these things were "too deep" for me. But while she combed and brushed my hair, Grandmother would really talk to me. She told me stories and recited dramatic readings from her youth. For Grandmother it was safe to speak the truth there behind my head, and I always knew by the rhythm and tug of the brushing when she was about to get "caught up in the spirit." That meant we were coming to a tough story, and now I knew to be especially still.

"It is April third, 1865, in Richmond, Virginia. Your great grandmother, Margaret Duke, is seven years old. Her father has gone fishing and she and her little sister, Vic, have gone into Richmond. They are playing when, suddenly, soldiers pour into the main street, breaking up the stores, breaking windows, busting open barrels of flour, pouring milk into the street. Margaret and her little sister are frightened. They sit down on the curb and they cry. A soldier breaks out of the melee and comes over to Margaret. He reaches in his pocket for a piece of hard tack. He bends down and hands it to Margaret and says, 'Little girl, stop crying. Go home and tell your people that they're free.'"

There is a pause in the brushing. I know Grandmother is going into her own pocket now, not for candy, but for her clean but scrumpled handkerchief to wipe away the silent tears. When the brushing begins again, it begins more gently. Now she is humming, nothing in particular, I think. When the humming subsides, the brushing subsides. "Even the hairs of your head are all numbered," she says quietly. And I know by the parable that she means that every hair is free. She told me many things I know she didn't plan to tell me.

. . . . . .

They'd just come out in the rhythm of the brushing.

Grandmother was good and healthy. She "kept herself up" as she would say admiringly about few others. But when she was in her eighties, Grandmother had a stroke, and she lost her speech. In the last weeks of Grandmother's life, my mother, who had kept up a constant vigil at Grandmother's hospital bedside, had to leave town for a few days. I lived nearby and was happy to take over the visits. As Grandmother was propped up there in her hospital bed, only her sweet side remained, and that just barely beneath the quiet surface. I knew that she would not want to appear unladylike in the company of the hospital staff, so I saw to it that her hair got combed and brushed and braided every day, just as she had done mine. And the miracle was that, as I stroked her hair in the familiar rhythms, the words to my own stories came forth. And in her eyes I read the words, "Did you get your lessons?" Yes, Grandmother, I got my lessons.

The September sky is blue and cloudless half a century later. It is a couple of ordinary weeks into the beginning of the fall semester at the seminary. Though it is still too early in the year for the school week to be supported by either habit or rhythm, there is buoyancy in the hopefulness of a new beginning. At two o'clock in the afternoon, we are showing up for class from places newly carved out in still ragged schedules. We take our places around the seminar table, pausing in our mutual greetings and shallow grumblings at the sound of the professor's voice.

"Well, here we are," says Pastor (as I call him), making gentle eye contact with each of us, gathering us in the unhurried sweep of his gaze. "The Lord be with you," he says, still collecting us in his vision. "And also with you," we say in a multi-toned voice echoing the myriad directions of our motley journeys. There follows a long, deep quiet. The noisiness, the business, the frantic stuff of schedules overly peopled with plans and regrets recedes. I feel the settling in, the gathering, the collective but uneven breathing in and out among us like leaky pistons hissing quietly out of phase with one another. Soft landings in the silence around the room signal the arrival of separate journeys into this moment of common destination. Then from deep within the silence, Pastor begins to pray, his voice resting on the outbreath of a bit of weariness of his own. God's Word is spoken and mercy reigns on the remnants of our rocky edges, scooping us up and holding us in this present-tense moment of refuge and strength: "O God, our times are in your hand."

"Sunday," Pastor announces, and the sunlight in the sound of the word brings the feeling of Sunday morning into the room. There is a pause while he appears to sort through his mind's library of Sundays, making choices from the volumes of Sundays stored there as his hands make a neat pile out of the already neat pile of volumes on the table in front of him. He leans forward on his elbows, and launches into a litany of Sunday images: the first day, the eighth day, the day of resurrection, the new sun, the Lord's Day, the day the community gathers. He invites us to remember our every Sundays aloud.

I hear the stories unfold around the seminar table, some raucous, some sad, some awkward, some distant, some weary. Some are irreverent, others quietly joyful. I am picturing the churches and Sunday-morning kitchen tables, the choir processions, and the full voices of one family sitting in the fourth pew back on the left every single week. I hear (and remember) the tension in the compromises made about going or not going to church in the stormy and questioning years of adolescence—however long or intermittent. Tables are being set for Sunday dinners and, over the familiar clamor of after-dinner dishes, I hear from some the monotonous roar of afternoon ball games on the TV. Someone reads the Sunday paper in the big red easy chair in front of a roaring fire. The sound of his snoring means he has fallen deep into a Sunday-afternoon postprandial snooze. I am taking in the images from the past, the texture and terrain of each journey when I hear Pastor ask, "Was there anyone who felt an obligation to go to church on Sunday?" Suddenly the Sunday-morning story I hear is the one awakening from a time inside of me.

✱ ✱ ✱

I am sitting in the dark brown, slippery wooden pew of St. Paul's, Spring Valley, comforted by knowing that my mother's purse contains a small supply of Lifesavers. My fingers are patrolling the corrugated edges of the funeral parlor fan that resides in the corner of the aisle end of the bench. Once in a while, I fan it open (slowly, so that its old, crispy folds won't creak too loudly.) As I do, a pink-cheeked, yellow-fleshed, three-quarter-view head of Jesus emerges from the folds, the letters S-N-I-F-F-I-N-S in lavender-lined gold forming a halo over his head. Having something to do with my fingers helps me to fix my attention on the images evoked by the constancy and familiarity of the service's choreography.

I don't literally understand much of what is being said, and I can't read the words in the little book. Though I am baffled by the strange string of phonics exercises that we recite in school as we stand by our buttoned-down desks, my grandmother has taught me how to run my finger from left to right along the words in the 1940 hymnal. So I look forward to the singing times when I can join in. But it is the actions themselves that are full of possibilities for my imagination and my dreams.

Held in the rhythm and flow, I keep a vigilant watch for the colors and textures, the smells and the sounds. I give each one a name and then name the feelings that rise up around them. I choose places on the landscape of my memory to store the images and the feelings which, when church is over, I will carry home to Grandmother. When I get back home, we will have church together.

Grandmother was always late. Not because she was old, but because it was just her habit.

· · · · ·

As a little girl, I just automatically thought of grandmothers as people who you waited for. It wasn't until I became a teacher myself that my mother told me that when Grandmother had school children "to see after," she was always on time for school. Grandmother was frequently too late for us to "carry" her to church on Sunday morning, though once in a while we'd try to trick her into being on time by telling her to be ready for the early service. But mostly she'd miss the trip. On those Sundays, when I got home from church, there was a different version of "Did I get my lessons?" Grandmother expected me to be able to tell her what the priest had said in his sermon. That seemed a little like cheating to me since that meant I had to sit up there and pay attention, and she didn't have to go at all. But the part I looked forward to was coming home and doing my own version of the preacher's sermon. The sermon Grandmother got was richly peopled by my imagination and far more dramatic than the original. When I finished my "rendition" (a word from the dramatic recitals of my grandmother's youth), Grandmother wanted me to play the hymns she'd missed. That was before I could read music, so I'd play by ear, banging the chords out on the black keys only with the piano pedal steadily down. Grandmother would sing out all the verses from the kitchen where, at one o'clock in the afternoon, she was just "getting" to her breakfast.

"On a day called Sunday there is a meeting in one place of those who live in the cities or the country and the memoirs of the apostles or the writings of the prophets are read as long as time permits."[1]

Back home with Grandmother, we are doing what people have done going back to the first centuries of gatherings in the synagogues and house churches of the Roman Empire. In our fierce hymnody, Grandmother and I echo generations of Sunday people, dragging

---

1 First Apology of Justin, 67. In *Early Christian Fathers*, Cyril C. Richardson, editor. (New York: Macmillan Publishing Co., 1970) p.287

our wearying stories of *chronos* to church. We are the lifting the voice of the people whose stories bear the wounds of chronological time. They are the wounds of pain, illness, death, humiliation, hunger, despair, fear. They are denials of our humanity and the protests against those denials that the world has chosen to ignore. They are the limitations we cannot accept in ourselves, the hurts we have dealt to others, and our sometimes insatiable need for forgiveness for our seemingly unforgivable separations from God in ourselves and others.

But our songs sing stories that carry our gifts too—our experiences, our dreams, our imaginations, our relationships with our parents, our grandparents, our children, and our friends. Our stories carry the gift of our searching, our longing, our memory of moments of God's saving grace. With those who go before us and beside us, with those who come willingly or reluctantly, we are processing to church to be unburdened.[2] Right here between the kitchen and the living room, we are gathering from the places of our myriad directions and motley journeys to participate in a feast hosted by the Holy Spirit—a feast of unforgetting.

The Word is "filled with the ancient longing for the day of God, that day understood as the time when tears will be wiped away and justice done."[3] Here, as Grandmother and I make church, the Word of God is spoken and mercy reigns on the remnants of our rocky edges, scooping us up and holding us in this present-tense moment of refuge and strength. "O God, our times are in your hand...."

Grandmother was always late in the ways measured by the clock. But with our stories in tow, here in our recreated after-church Sunday assembly, *chronos* becomes *kairos*. "The Word

2 Thomas Merton, "Time and Unburdening and the recollection of the Lamb: The Easter Service in Faulkner's The Sound and the Fury" (Trustees of the Merton Library)

3 Gordon W. Lathrop. Homily for Proper 25, Cycle C in *Homilies for the Christian People*, Cycles ABC. Gail Ramshaw, editor (Collegeville, MN.: The Liturgical Press, 1991) p.531

. . . . . .

of God breaks into time.... It reveals the beginning and the ending: the meaningless of time and the full meaning of time."[4]

In the poetry of Howard Thurman: *"The commonplace is shot through now with new glory— old burdens become lighter, deep and ancient wounds lose much of their hurting. A crown is placed over our heads that for the rest of our lives we are trying to grow tall enough to wear."*[5]

In the presence of the remembered Word, we sit on the children's chair between God's knees and wait for the pull and tug of God's fierce passion going at the knotty problems of our lives. When the story has been told, there is a pause. A grieving God is going into Her pocket for a handkerchief "to wipe away every tear." We sit in the lap of God's time and hear the Word of ever-loving promise: "Even the hairs on your head are counted," whispers God, "and every hair is free."

✳ ✳ ✳

On a blue and cloudless Sunday morning three decades after Grandmother's death, I stand before Jacob Epstein's huge bronze portrait of "Social Consciousness" high above the tree line on the back steps of the Philadelphia Art Museum. A woman seated between mercy and strength draws me to her. Her arms, raised against the sky, invite me to pull up between her knees. Now she calls, and though I'm amazed she would be calling me, my feet seem to move toward her with a memory of their own. As I get closer I can hear her singing. *"God is our refuge and strength, a very present help in trouble. Therefore we will not fear, though the earth be moved, and though the mountains be toppled into the depths of the sea."* In her voice I hear my grandmother's voice. Or is it God's voice?

---

4 Thomas Merton, p.14

5 Howard Thurman. *The Mood of Christmas* (Richmond, IN.: Friends United Press, 1985) pp.10,11

There is a pause when, for a moment, I hear no sound, and for fear of missing something, I make no sound of my own. *"There is a river whose streams make glad the city of God."* She is singing again. No, she is weeping. But these are tears of joy. These are the rain of *kairos*, the tears of fullness and peace. I am in the lap of God's time.

I take a few steps down from her, but turn back for one more look. The inscription below her feet gives me something to hold on to: *"Social Consciousness: A grand, sane, towering, seated Mother, Chair'd in the adamant of Time."*[6] Adamant of Time. Adamant. Insistent. Tough. Unyielding against the odds. As I am walking away, I hear her call after me in my grandmother's voice, "OOooo! Is that you, Pauloo? Did you get your lessons today?" I hear the call, and I know I'd better take up the challenge.

Weeks before, Pastor had asked whether any of us had felt an obligation to go to church on Sunday. Now the story that was awakened in me then is revealing God's purpose. The word "adamant" is first a noun referring to a legendary impenetrable rock.[7] The church is that rock calling me to the permanence and the refuge of its lap, to sit at the crossing where I will receive the burdened stories and tell the Story of the fullness of God's justice and mercy. I am called to church to bathe and to set and bless its table. And I am called in the adamant of time to teach.

I know that because there are people in places begging for the reign of *kairos*, I will have to carry God's lap out into the world. There, with Grandmother at my side, we will have church. I will remember the important lessons of life she taught me: serious bathing, pay attention in church, set the table after bath, always make an extra place, sit down and share

---

6 Walt Whitman. " America" in *Leaves of Grass*, (New York, N.Y.: Modern Library) p. 395

7 William Morris, editor. *The American Heritage Dictionary of the English Language* (Boston, MA.: Houghton Mifflin Co., 1978)

a cup of pot liquor. And because a lot of Grandmother's rules were about the way we spoke, and especially the way we spoke to her, I trust that I will dare to speak for God when I say, "Even the hairs of your head are all counted, and every one is free."

Not long after that blue and cloudless morning, I came across a letter written to me by Grandmother in the spring of my senior year of college. In the eighth decade of her life, she still had schoolgirl handwriting. Folded into the letter was a frayed ten dollar bill.

1967 -   *Jan. 15th*   *21 yrs.*

My dear Paula,

> *You are with us at last. You say "What do you mean?" Why! You are 20 + 1 yrs. They say you are a woman. Is it so, or are you still hunting for other things for which you are hunting to finish the definition? I'll leave it to you to answer. Anyhow, it is a great pleasure to be writing you just a little previous to this day of days. May you have not those 21 yrs but 21 + 21 + 21 + 21 yrs. and more.*

Congratulations to you and your parents

I love you all,

Grandmother Morgan

Get what you would like

Excuse illegibility and mistakes wherever they occur, as I am doing this against great odds.

. . . . . .

4

We are climbing Jacob's ladder.
We are climbing Jacob's ladder.
We are climbing Jacob's ladder, Soldiers of the cross.
Every rung goes higher, higher.
Every rung goes higher, higher.
Every rung goes higher, higher, Soldiers of the cross.

IT IS 1949, SOMEWHERE in the undercroft of St. Martin's Church in Harlem. The girls and boys sit around two low rectangular tables pushed together to make a very big square table. The teacher is very tall and skinny and severe in her navy suit. Her huge-brimmed navy blue hat and the fact that she doesn't sit down make her seem like a giant and give this going-on-four-year-old a deep feeling of dread. The rule is that whenever the word "Jesus" is spoken, you have to bow your head. If you break the rule, the teacher comes up in back of you and bows it for you with an un-gentle swat. (It's only now looking back that I realize that's why she couldn't sit down.) She is on the lookout for rule breakers. Some of the boys break the rule on purpose just to see the old gal fly around the room. When she has at them, they bob and weave with an expertise that I secretly admire.

The Sunday school book illustrations of the kingdom make first-century Galilee out to look like Dick and Jane and Sally and Spot and Puff's neighborhood, except instead of having a mother, these children are happily romping around the feet of a pink-cheeked, long-haired, sandal-footed stranger. Everyone in the picture is the same color—the color the Crayola company calls "flesh."

I am a stranger in this kingdom that has no brown-skinned people, no grandmothers

· · · · · ·

who teach, no women doctors like my mother, nor fathers like mine who make their children's lunches and sing spirituals as the children fall asleep in his arms. I am skeptical of this kingdom that has no hospitals or city streets, no people sleeping over heat vents in the dead of winter—in fact, no winters at all, no poor people, no sick people, no troubled people, no sad people. These do not look like the people I see every day with my own eyes. "Suffer the little children," says the illustration. Suffer the little children. Why were we going to suffer, I wonder silently. The feeling I am having now I name "suffer" and store it in a special place in my heart where it becomes part of the hidden reality of a lifetime of seeking to act against people who would make other people suffer.

When my time came, and it came at an early age, I became a sojourner in school where I would soon learn that school did not invite or welcome the gifts of intuition and imagination which fueled the world I lived in outside of school, any more than its Sunday school counterpart. Nor was the story they were telling at school any closer to the truth about the blur of a world that passed the steamy bus window as we traveled to and fro. I was "school-worthy" enough to learn quickly how to memorize what the teachers said and to store the often unrelated information in my brain long enough to dish it back on a test. I had to learn to take what they were droning on about in pale, strident voices and transform it into something I could actively engage in, something I could fuel with my curiosity, intuition and imagination. "What happens next?" I was wondering, "What is the rest of the story?" I had to create my own teachable moments in a school system that rewarded only rote memory and the ability to fill in the blanks.

In school, I used up much of my intuition and creative energy adapting to the relentless string of discontinuities I faced between who I was inside and the person I needed to be on the outside in order to survive in school. I quickly learned to rechannel my intuitive energy from intellectual and creative endeavors to "reading" my teachers, to knowing how to respond the way they expected. At school I had to unremember who I was, what my story was, and become someone else in order to survive. And the horror of it was, that, like most children, I was very good at it.

Our parents were very involved in our schooling, and supported our adventures at school in every possible way. They showed up at every sporting event, every speech we gave or concert we played in. My dad had an enormous and infectious laugh, and it never took too long to know where he was sitting in a crowd, and my mom was always next to him. I marveled, when I became a parent myself, at how they managed with very busy work lives to always be there; but they had been sojourners all of their lives, and operated with passion, hope, and the knowledge that nobody but them would protect their children in school.

Advocating for us at school meant that Mom and Dad were fierce critics of the school system. They were advocates of justice and peace in the world at a time when we regularly had to duck under our desks during air raid drills at school. They stood up for my brother and sister who stood up to a bullying "citizens' education" teacher who had tried to push me under my desk when I resisted first his orders and then his verbal threats. My father hated the way we were deprived of learning about our African-American heritage in school, though that was just more cause to tell our story at home. He got himself elected to the school board and among many other things, fought the use of textbooks that denied our people's existence.

When I was called in with my parents by the small-minded eighth grade guidance counselor who announced to us that I was "not college material" and that he was putting me in the non-academic track, my parents threw body and soul in harm's way. Small-minded, bullying people in school and in the world were their enemies, and in our house, the unspoken translation of the gospel "love your enemy" was *teach your enemy*. Recently, I found out from my mother that each one of the Lawrence children had the experience of being told we were "not college material." Maybe that has something to do with the fact that we all have vocations teaching people to teach their enemy.

The story we were learning at school was played against the story we learned as our family went on peace marches and civil rights marches and people in the movement filled our home and sat at our table with their stories, which was our story. We were not to be deprived of these treasures just because school was not ready to take care of them.

In the evening, at the dinner table, my brother and sister delighted in my devastating imitations of our hapless teachers, egging me on by calling out requests and cueing me with lines they knew would bring big, old Dizzy or Mr. Boozer or Prof instantly to life. I'd have at these poor suckers until we'd laughed ourselves up a storm. "You're going to hurt yourself, Paula Jean," my father would say, trying to regain some measure of dinnertime decorum. "If we can't think of anything nice to say, let's not say anything at all," my mother would add, trying to bring the semi-hysteria to a semi-close. But both of them somehow knew that, as hard as we were on our teachers, school was harder on us. We destroyed our teachers at home so we could survive the destruction of school. "Do you understand?" I imitate the teacher up in my face, then turning to play myself, I dutifully nod my head "yes." What I really understand is that it's best to keep these pearls of understanding hidden on the landscape of my memory and in my heart, where they will not be mauled and trampled underfoot. Years later, as a teacher, I would remember that feeling when I saw in the eyes of children words from a poem by Madeleine L'Engle:

. . . . . .

She explodes with joy.
Sparks of gold and diamond fly
from the tips of her fingers
and her dancing toes.
Her laugh is like a crystal ball
and yet it has the earthy healthiness
of blades of sun-ripe wheat.

She implodes
with sorrow.
She takes within her all the gold,
the diamonds and the sunny laughter.
Deep, deep within herself she goes
And hides the pain
protects it in her heart;
talks like an ordinary day
except the sun has gone
and the sky is blue.

Who knows
what thoughts she hides from herself?
she keeps her sorrow,
and the scars
are underneath the flesh
unseen, enclosed within the shell.
The hidden grain of anguish
may one day turn into a pearl.[1]

1 Madeleine L'Engle. *Charlotte* from *Weather of the Heart* (Colorado Springs, CO: Water Brook Press, 2001).

***

It is the last week in August, forty years later. I have started my round of opening-of-the-year school visits—five cities in six days. I love my work. Each school I visit is a new adventure, a chance to add to my collection of stories, a new opportunity to teach and to learn. The traveling itself admittedly makes me weary. I have learned, after a few years of being on the road much of the time, to carry plenty of evidence of home with me: a collection of family pictures to set up by my bedside, a candle for the side of the tub while I take a hot soak at the end of the day, and of course our own house brand of soap. Our magnificent telephone bill reflects the ritual nightly calls home. I am calling to check on possible news from our sojourning sons. I am calling to complain about my day. I am calling to record the triumphs. I am calling to ask for advice, for wisdom, for the perspective of distance. And I am calling to hear about the triumphs, to listen to complaints, to give advice, to hold the phone to my ear and gather strength even from the silence which itself is a connection to home. And though he left this earth several years ago, I can still see Stuart, our loving and faithful golden dog sitting by the door he saw me leave by three days ago, ever hopeful of my imminent return.

I am a teacher, and like generations before me and beside me, a sojourner in schools. I have learned that *ger*, the Hebrew word for sojourner, means stranger within the gates, and that ancient Hebrew law protected sojourners from harm. For twenty-five years I have been wandering across the land, and through these gates, finding lost children, mining for their strengths. I stand at the door of the school with all those whose stories have called me over the threshold, echoing the question I still hold in my heart: "Will anybody know who I am?"

She is the seventh-grade child who has just moved from a city far away, doesn't know what the deal is, doesn't know where to sit in the cafeteria, seems to her the groups are formed and she'll never have a friend.

She is the quiet, centered, competent, even, soft-spoken, African-American girl who the other kids' parents find mysterious. Then her mystery becomes their fear, blamed on her for what is held privately inside of her. "I find her threatening," says one parent to another.

They are the loud, locker-slamming, up-in-your-face angry kids from the other side of town. The talk among some of the faculty is that if you bring them in line, you'll get called a bigot.

She is the brown-skinned three-year-old who brings a drawing home the first day of school. She has made her parents and her brother brown, and has used the peach crayon for herself. "God made a mistake," she says, "all the other girls are peach."

He is the Black custodian whose children have gone through the school. His grandchild is in the first grade. Members of the teaching faculty are called by their surnames and titles. He is called by his first name, and insists, without looking at you when you offer, that he doesn't mind either way. She is his granddaughter.

She is the African-American teacher who went to segregated schools in a nearby county. She remembers the warmth and love of the all-Black school full of church people and the people who did her hair and sold groceries to her family—people that felt like family. She remembers 1954, the year of *Brown vs. Board of Education*, as a time of victory but also profound loss as she was sent off to the white school. The teacher wouldn't call on her no matter how long she held her hand up. "I thought I might be invisible," she says, standing before me now, telling her story forty years later, still holding her hand up in the air.

She is the mother who rode her childhood school bus with all of the Black children from her rural Georgia town, who tells me how she held her breath in fear as the bus clattered by the all-white school. She tells me that she has had to learn to suspend her fears as her own child daily walks through the door of a mostly white independent school. "I am still holding my breath," she says quietly.

He is the veteran schoolteacher in a high-powered, suburban school district in the Northeast. He wonders aloud how students nowadays lost their respect for their elders, and then in the same breath, he recalls the tight-knit community of his South Carolina seacoast childhood. "People would walk two miles on their aching feet to tell your mother you did something wrong," he tells me.

He is the seventy-year-old man who cannot read, who has the courage to daily cross the threshold of the after-school tutorial program and there with children one tenth his age, syllable by mysterious syllable he discovers a new world. She is the young teacher who sits by his side absorbing the gift of wisdom.

They are the silent ones, the loud ones, the eager ones, the talented ones, the angry ones, the ones who stayed in school and the ones who left, but whose stories we may never know.

I stand at the door of the school remembering that I come from generations of sojourners whose historical memory called them through these gates, who held the hands of their children and grandchildren as they walked through, and who are here beside me now calling me through the gates to teach.

It is late August, and even the little symbolic comforts of home that I have brought along in my suitcase are wearying under the strain of these fine school adventures. I know it is time to pause and welcome the healing presence of the stories that unfold as I walk back over the paths that lead me home to the gift in myself. The stories that unfold from within are clear, cool water for the thirsty sojourner.

It is late in the evening of the family's dinner celebration of my birthday. After a day filled with birthday celebrations with school and neighborhood friends and birthday supper with the family, after bath and pajama time, all tucked in between the clean sheets, Mom sits on the side of my bed and tells me the story of the family getting ready for me to be born. I can see her leaning slightly forward with her elbows on her knees, telling the story as if it has never been told before. In fifty-five birthdays, Mom has never missed the moment of this story's telling, and though for the last thirty-five years or so I have heard it on the telephone, I can still feel her sitting on the edge of my bed, the story invoked like a familiar psalm.

"It was late in the winter of 1945. Grandma Lettie, your father's mother, was downstairs. Brave and strong she was, but her life was ebbing out. She had no sad words for herself. Brother Chuck she knew. Pride she had in her switch-a-bottom Sally. She wanted to know Paula, but here you were to be deprived of immediate knowledge of Lettie. Grandma Lettie left you a part of herself, an inheritance, an opal ring. I was responsible for saving it for you to be given to you at the time of your engagement to be married, that you might know your wealth from the Lawrence side, of which the opal was a symbol. To my sorrow, the opal ring disappeared from the desk drawer on the trip north from Nashville to New York. Amidst all the travail, you were born. This must be a part of your caring, loving self, 'the little therapist,' as your nursery school teacher called you. You were life out of death, but not a replacement, which any able-bodied human being quite naturally resents and resists."

My parents, feeling I should have tangible evidence of my inheritance, replaced the symbol with a ring just like the original, and they gave it to me on the night of our engagement. Some years later, our young family was robbed, and of all the television and stereo junk that was taken, the ring was the only thing I really lost. My parents went to New Zealand the next year and found an opal. They brought it back and had it set in silver to match my wedding ring, and I wear it still to remind me that the refrain of the birth-night story still comes: *This is the sign of the strength passed on to you through the struggle.*

· · · · · ·

I know that as my mother tells this story, as the images and sounds awaken in her, the pain of former struggles comes out of the past and into the present. But with that pain comes the remembrance of the strength given as an inheritance from grandmother to mother to daughter, over and over again on the day of her birth and healing.

✱ ✱ ✱

It is spring of 1988, a Saturday afternoon. I am baking bread in the still somewhat unfamiliar kitchen of the home we moved into only a few months ago. There is a long-distance call from my mom, one of those calls I have come to look forward to as a visit from a close friend.

"I've just been looking around at all the gifts you have given me," she says. And as she says it, I picture the double heart-shaped wooden frame I made with a jigsaw when I was ten. I had pasted pictures of my mom and dad on the back of each heart so that when they showed through, they were looking at each other. I had given it to them for their anniversary. I imagine Mom is glancing down at the frame on the little desk in the dining room. Or maybe she is phoning from the bedroom and looking over at the beads I'd made her in Girl Scouts. They are hanging over her mirror. Or maybe Mom is in Dad's study looking out into the hallway at a painting I'd painted one summer during college. These were the gifts I imagine she is talking about. But Mom surprises me when she tells me she is talking about a very different kind of gift. What Mom tells me then brings a more recent image to mind, the image of an April day two years before.

It is a week after my father's death, after the trumpets and choirs and bishops and priests and deacons and family and friends have celebrated his great and full life in a wonderful send-off in the cathedral in New York. After the neighbors, who have plied us with casseroles and salads and loaves of bread have gone home, after grandchildren have returned to Boston

· · · · · ·

and Philadelphia and San Francisco, my brother and sister and I awaken early into the April morning quiet of the house we grew up in. Our mother has awakened even earlier, and has already had her coffee at the dining room table, breaking the silence only to speak to a purple finch who appears at the dining room window. She has gone off to her office on the other side of the house, but first has left us a note on the table that, as always, begins, "Dear Ones."

What follows is a list of things Mom needs our help with. It is not unlike the hundreds of other Saturday morning lists left over the years on the dining room table. She needs my lawyer brother's help at the bank and sorting through some insurance matters. She's asked my sister and me to work on clearing out my Great Aunt Hazel's old room. My father's closet needs going through, and the freezer needs some attention. So we spend one glorious day with our sleeves rolled up, digging through the things that need doing. And the wonderful work is punctuated by side-splitting laughter when my sister and I find, at the bottom of one of Aunt Hazel's old purses, a big wad of ancient dollar bills tied up in a rubber band with a label in our great aunt's old-fashioned hand that says, "For Brandy." "Let's not tell the others!" whispers my sister in mock secrecy that reminds me of the sisterly conspiracies we had as kids. And just then, from across the hall in my parents' room, the sounds of my brother's weeping. He has found some every-day evidence of my dad in the pocket of one of his suits. As the day goes on like that, we all keep expecting our dad to call us to the table for one of his delicious home-made soups.

By day's end, Sara, Chuck and Mom have gathered around the fire in the living room, ready to put this day to rest. But I have still one more thing I have the urge to do. I need to straighten my mother's jewelry. I used to do this as a child. The beautiful wooden box we gave her for her seventieth birthday, the assorted baskets and containers, the wooden box my brother made in second grade, are filled with Mom's wonderful jewelry—necklaces and rings and pins and earrings and hairpins, put back after a tired day—are fairly scrambled and beg my urge to organize them. "Come on, Paula Jean," my mother calls from the living room, but I have just come to that final major knot. It looks like a real challenge, but untying knots is my specialty. This is where a store of patience and faith and agile fingers has never let me down. So I sit on the edge of the bed examining the ancient knot, looking for the origin of the strands, working the loops loose, releasing little bits of old chain. As I gently push, thread, turn, and release the ancient stuff, I am thinking how much like my work at school this is—knots in children's shoelaces, knots in the thread of a stitchery project, knots in the scheduling, knots of misunderstanding, knots of history entangled for years before I ever arrived. And there at work, too, I examine the knots, looking for the origin of the strands, gently but firmly pushing at the tangles, trying to remember not to pull because pulling makes it worse, all the while knowing the store of patience and faith that it can be done and feeling the nimble fingers, and, most of all, having the urge to have the knots untied. In the end, one last entanglement opens quietly in my hands. I lay the jewelry down in the boxes and go sit by my father's fire with my father's family.

Two years later, my mother has called to say, "I've just been looking around at all the gifts you've given me. You untied all those knots for me." Suddenly I have a surge of knowing myself as one who has a gift for untying knots.

✷ ✷ ✷

"I will not leave you orphaned," Jesus tells his disciples. *"The Holy Spirit will teach you all things and remind you of all I have said."*[2]

---

2 John 14: 18, 26

It is the fall of 1991. Five years after my father's death, I am standing in a crowded school lobby following a concert given by Ashley Bryan, an African-American author, musician and illustrator of children's books. I am waiting in the crush of mostly white, well-healed people to get my book signed. I don't want to be here with these people who don't understand the beautiful images and voices he has given us. Though more than forty years have gone by since my first sojourns into Dick and Jane's neighborhood, tonight I feel the pain of being alienated in school all over again.

Brown-skinned third grade Kristi *is* Harriet Tubman, the principal tells me. And I can see the way she has her little "slaves" all lined up in a row (five little boys—four are white and one is Black). She has the spirit of Harriet Tubman's discipline. "If we're gonna be free, you must fall into my line and do what I say," she tells them. "Eenie, Meenie, Minie, Mo," she points, "Catch a 'something' by the toe," I can't hear what's being caught by the toe. Or maybe it is just too painful to remember.

What I do remember with all the teacher in me is that the moment of pain is the teachable moment. I catch her eye and ask if her name is Harriet Tubman. We trade giggles and then real names. She insists hers is Kristi. "Kristi Tubman, then," I say. And by this time she is thoroughly tucked under my wing. I don't remember how she got there.

She smells like the first, fresh chew-taste of bubble gum; and since it is a smell I like (and was almost never privileged to taste firsthand as a child) I say so. "What have you been eating that smells so good?" I ask.

"I don't know," she says. Then I realize it is the smell of her hair oil.

"Oh, I know, it's the smell of your hair oil," I comment matter-of-factly, letting her know that I am familiar with *our* hair. "What's it called?"

She has to tell me three times before I get that she's saying "*Let's Jam*," and I make a mental note that it is the 1990s version of hair jelly.

· · · · · ·

"Do they let people over forty-six wear it?" I ask, and we're both in giggles again. She is still under there rocking back and forth to a tune heard only by the two of us, I think, when I know the moment has come to venture forth where only guardian angels would tread.

"When you did *Eenie Meenie Minie Mo*, what did you catch by the toe?" I ask. She is still tucked under my wing.

Bouncing in her own rhythm now, she sings out, "Eenie, Meenie, Minie, Mo, catch a *pixie* by the toe."

"Hmmm, pixie," I say. "You know, when we were growing up, we weren't supposed to say that rhyme."

"Why?" she asks, still tucked under my wing.

"Because the original word was not 'pixie'. Do you know what it was?"

"Lion? Catch a lion by the toe?" Ashley Bryan is looking at us over his half glasses.

"No," I say, the pain rising up now into my throat. "No, but close. It was 'tiger,' but people said 'tigger.' What they really meant was something awful that rhymes with 'tigger,' something that would hurt our feelings."

"What?" she asks now, no longer comfortably under my wing but looking me square in the eye for what she knows but can't believe.

And now as I see her jaw drop in shock, I am remembering where I stood at the kitchen counter as a little girl when my father, hearing that I'd brought that rhyme home from school, taught me that same history lesson. And then, remembering what he taught me next, I said, "In my family, we used *One Potato Two Potato.*[3]" Then I took my friend into our little circle, and taught her how. And as I did, the pain lifted, as it always does when we know ourselves in the teachable moment.

---

3 I was reminded of this family history by my brother, Charles R. Lawrence III, in "If He Hollers Let Him Go: Regulating Racist Speech on Campus", from *Duke Law Journal: Volume 3, 1990.*

Ashley Bryan signs my book, "For Paula Jean, A child is born. Behold that star!"

✱ ✱ ✱

In this quiet place years ago,
my family knelt down and caught a glimpse of the eternal.
We left our markers in the soil
in memory of the families
who once lived here.[4]

The beautiful, lilting young female voice tells us the story of generations of a Gullah family on the South Carolina and Georgia Sea Islands portrayed in Julie Dash's film, *Daughters of the Dust.* This great-granddaughter's voice speaks and I hear my own story. I know others must hear theirs too.

We were children of those who chose to survive.
Years later, my Momma told me
she knew I had been sent forward by the old souls.[5]

It is late November, and I have begun to think about the invitation to address a gathering of educators from all over the country, a meeting of school principals in the Georgia Sea Islands in February. I am excited to be going on this particular sojourn. I read everything I can find about the history of the islands, but I haven't found so much. A full seven years after his death, I am missing my dad. He was the family historian, the *griot*—the rememberer and teller of the family history. I am suddenly sabotaged by sadness, resentful all over again of how much focus and attention and energy from my teenage years was spent adapting and fitting in at school at a time when I know Dad must have longed to tell me these stories of our African beginnings.

4 Julie Dash. *Daughters of the Dust*

5 Julie Dash. *Daughters of the Dust*

So I fix a cup of tea, and settle by the kitchen telephone for what I know will be an extended visit with my mother. My mother has the kind of memory I have—a feeling memory—and we talk around it and up on it until we make a landing on some profoundly important connection. (I think she must have been a lot like me in school.) "Yes," she says, "I see by your itinerary that you are off to the Sea Islands." Mom is like an air traffic controller, keeping all of her children's schedules by the telephone on the kitchen counter. "What is your topic?" she asks, and when I tell her "Sojourners: Strangers within the Gates," she says, "Where did I read something about a little school in the Sea Islands? Just a minute," and the phone has clunked down.

I hear the sounds of home in the background and am attacked by a mild case of the blues, wishing I could be sitting there by the fireplace. Just then Mom is back. "I don't know what became of my glasses," she says. "I'm using your father's glasses. They were right here by the phone." Seven years later and they are still swapping glasses. I always imagined there was some magic in that, and maybe there is, because suddenly Mom is reading from a little pamphlet—the story I know my father would have told us by heart.

Two hundred years ago, West Africans were wrenched from their rice-growing lands and were brought in chains to these islands. Slaves became the backbone of the rice culture here off the coast of Georgia. They tended the indigo and the "Sea Island cotton." After the Civil War, the islands were taken over by northern white industrialists. Freed peoples of color worked in exchange for wages used to buy parcels of land. Hurricanes and the boll weevil eventually sent the Northerners packing, enabling the Gullah peoples to maintain, in the beauty and isolation of the Sea Islands, the African culture. Children were given "basket names" such as Rain and Hardtimes and Handful. The Gullah buried their dead by the water so that their souls could go back to Africa. Later another wave of industry—this time the resort industry—displaced many of these souls— living and dead. [6]

6 paraphrased from an article by Joyce Hollyday ("A Plague in Paradise") in *Sojourners*, August-September, 1992, p.14, p.16

. . . . . .

Mom reads on about a little school for the freed people of color started by wealthy white ladies from the North.

First it was the young African mothers who went to the school with their children at their knees. Then when they knew it was okay, they sent just their children. The school became the center of social and political activity for the island. Later, in the 60's, it served as a training center for civil rights activities, and Martin Luther King, Jr. and his people would use this little school for a retreat. [7]

Mom says, "Let me know when to stop reading," but my heart is already pounding, thinking about my own sojourn to the Sea Islands. I am practically dancing to Alice Walker's poem. It is a poem I said daily when I was the principal of a school because it kept me knowing what sojourn I was on:

> *They were women then*
> *My mama's generation*
> *Husky of voice - Stout of*
> *Step*
> *With fists as well as*
> *Hands*
> *How they battered down*
> *Doors*
> *And ironed*
> *Starched white*
> *Shirts*
> *How they led*
> *Armies*

---

7 Ibid p.16

Headragged Generals

Across mined

Fields

Booby-trapped

Ditches

To discover books

Desks

A place for us

How they knew what we

Must know

Without knowing a page

Of it

Themselves.[8]

It is Sunday, February twenty-first. I have landed at the Jacksonville airport, all baggage accounted for. A young, African-American stewardess on the plane has seen me looking over a review of *Daughters of the Dust* and engages me in welcome chatter about the movie—what I think, what her girlfriend thinks, what her girlfriend's boyfriend thinks, what she thinks. She has an article from *Essence* magazine in her bag. It's about the Georgia Sea Islands. She'll let me "hold it" she tells me, reminding me that you can't get *Essence* at every airport. I take her presence as a good sign for my sojourn. On the airport-to-hotel limousine, I keep seeing this African-American woman's pretty face, and feeling the buoyancy of the connection we made.

---

8 Alice Walker. *Revolutionary Petunias and Other Poems.* (New York, N.Y.: Harcourt Brace Jovanovich, Inc. 1973.)

· · · · · ·

Now we are crossing a bridge and I am straining to see signs of the story I have come here to be a part of. Nothing. I see nothing but highway butting up against marsh. Then suddenly we stop. We are here. But I am terribly disoriented. This is not the beautiful natural stretch of the Sea Islands of my roots. This is a very fancy resort. This is a palace. This is a mansion. No. This is a plantation.

My school colleagues are already here, browner than their usual school selves, the quick work of the resort sun. They are greeting me warmly, but I can't quite know them because I don't know myself at this moment. I hear my own voice as if it is six thousand miles away: *Yes, I'm fine. Yes, it is a lovely location. Yes, it's good to get away.* I decide to say I am simply overwhelmed. That won't hurt anyone's feelings.

Sunday evening I call home. John, who is called to this Sea Island soil by his vocation as a geologist, listens to my hurt and longing and desperation. Then he tells me, "Get up and go out to the beach in the morning, and remember that two hundred million years ago, there was no gap between Africa and where you are standing. It was all one." "So I might be standing on a few grains of Africa?" I ask him hopefully. "A few grains," he says generously. And I fall off to sleep.

In the morning I wake up not knowing where I am. I turn my head slowly on this soft, comfortable pillow. What is that I see? The hotel-decorator picture over my bed is a slave cabin with the "darkies" happily singing and dancing. "No," I say aloud to no one. (Years of practicing denial in schools.) "No," I say again. But it is.

"By the waters of Babylon we sat down and wept when we remembered Zion."[9] I am saying that psalm of the exiled Hebrew sojourners when I remember what my parents practiced in the face of small-minded, bullying people: *teach your enemy.* Teach those who hurt you.

---

9 Psalm 137:1

Teach those who don't understand you. Teach those who don't see your pain or choose to ignore it. Teach those who, with no intention of malice, strip you of your dignity. Teach. And so it falls to the sojourner, the stranger within the gates, to teach.

And so I taught, just as I always have. I taught them the story of the sojourner. I taught them my story. And as I taught, I felt the healing begin again.

✳ ✳ ✳

"Jacob left Beer-sheba and went toward Haran. He came to a certain place and stayed there for the night, because the sun had set. Taking one of the stones of the place, he put it under his head and lay down in that place. And he dreamed that there was a ladder set up on earth, the top of it reaching to heaven; and the angels of God were ascending and descending on it. And God stood beside him and said, 'Know that I am with you and will keep you wherever you go, and will bring you back to this land; for I will not leave you until I have done what I have promised you.'" [10]

It is late on a winter afternoon my first year of seminary. I have cloistered myself in the over-heated stacks of the seminary library and have, as always, surrounded myself with an overly ambitious pile of texts. I have read and reread this sentence in whatever theological tome I am supposed to be digesting in preparation for tomorrow's exam. As I begin to give in to the urge to put my head wearily down on the book, I am recalling, not the ancient theological concept before me, but a home-grown theology practiced by my teacher grandmother. When Grandmother felt she could not get something "across to a child," for example, his or her "figures," she would say, "I need to sleep on it." Then she would take the arith-

10 Genesis 28: 10-12, 15

metic book and put it under her pillow. In the morning, she would know how she was going to teach her student.

And so, like my grandmother before me, I make the stony, old book my pillow, and lay my head down on it. Soon I am falling asleep and dreaming that I am in the stacks of the old Swarthmore College library of a quarter century before. Stalactites and stalagmites inhabit my little study cave in a dark, musty corner of this numbingly serious place. Deposits of some other sort layered on the would-be window render it nearly opaque. I seem to have given up on whatever this is I am studying, an organic chemistry problem written in Hebrew, I think. All twenty-two consonants and a million little mysterious vowel points and rules are tumbling in fragments out of my brain and onto the library floor. I am utterly overwhelmed. So I put my head down on the book and fall asleep. Here in the dream within the dream, I see the answer to the problem carved in the stone pillow under my head: *"Genesis 28:16."* I translate the letters with ease, and then fall into a deep and restful sleep. Soon someone's familiar, big, hand is gently tapping on my head. Then whoever is there beside me says in a familiar voice, "I love you, Paula Jean."

"Then Jacob woke from his sleep and said, 'Surely God is in this place, and I did not know it.'"[11]

---

11 Genesis 28:16

5

I'm gonna sit at the welcome table.
I'm gonna sit at the welcome table one of these days, Hallelujah.
I'm gonna sit at the welcome table.
I'm gonna sit at the welcome table one of these days.

OUR HOUSE HAD A DIFFERENT SOUND on Sunday mornings. There was a different feeling in the air. I slept with my curtains opened so that the morning sun, coming over the hills and through the woods, was the first to awaken me. On rainy Sundays, the wind would brush the tree branches against the wall of the house. The rain itself, first gentle then pelting harder, was my wake-up call. Occasionally our long-haired black cat had stayed out all night and, knowing I had a soft heart for his late-night sojourns, he would rattle at the door that opened from the woods into my room. If I didn't awaken to the annoying sound of his insistent paws pulling at the screen, our loving Irish setter would rise from his place on the rug next to my bed, nestle his wet, warm nose under my chin, and lovingly lift me from my sleep.

Sundays were different. I could lie in bed on Sundays, staring out into the trees and the purple and amber light of the morning. The designs in the tree branches, the sounds in the wind, the smell of the morning air were backdrops for my wondering, for the dreams that came from my sleep into the light of day.

And now the clanging of pans from the kitchen begins to penetrate my morning reverie, signaling that my father is up and making Sunday pancakes. There is no known recipe for these fantastic concoctions, and I hear cupboard doors being opened and shut as my father gets ideas about what he wants to throw into this Sunday's batch. He cooks the way

· · · · · ·

someone else would conduct an orchestra—waving in the flour with his left hand, crashing open the eggs on the side of the bowl with his right, bringing in the oil as he pours with the spout first close to the bowl then high above it. Something for leavening gets tossed in in undetermined amounts. Then time to cue in the spice shelf. Now it's anybody's guess. The conductor might be in the mood for nutmeg ground freshly from the whole bean. Maybe a little sugar for browner cakes. Now for the surprises—always surprises: slices of banana, pecans, and peaches in season. He whips the mix to an allegro tempo, and when it is orchestrated to his satisfaction, he raps the wooden spoon on the side of the bowl as the conductor would rap the baton on the stand. This signals readiness. I know the next rap will be on my door. It will be an invitation to rise and eat, to partake of the delicious day. "Christ Is Risen!" he booms out in his trumpeter's voice, already fully jubilant so early in the morning. "He is risen indeed," I manage from beneath the coziness of my covers. It is Sunday morning—time to Keep the Feast.

"Behold, I stand at the door and knock, says the Lord. If you hear my voice and open the door, I will come into the house and eat with you, and you with me."[1]

I hear the invitation, and I have returned to the table of my childhood. My place at the family table—down at the end next to my father, my back to the window, Grandfather and Grandmother across, my brother and sister on the same side and my mother down at the far end—was where I began to carve out my place in the world. This is where I had my first lessons in being a daughter, a granddaughter, a sister to a sister and a sister to a brother (which are two different things). At the table, we waged our complaints about life. We wore

---

1 "Antiphon At the Entrance" from "Celebration for a Home" *The Book of Occasional Services* (New York, N.Y.: Church Hymnal Corporation) 1995

. . . . . .

grooves in the family arguments, laughed at the family jokes, and told and retold the family story. Sometimes the stories my grandparents told of life in the deeply segregated South were so tough and so filled with rage, that my parents changed the subject or took us young ones temporarily out of hearing's way. Though these moments always filled me with confusion and pain, it was from these stories that I first learned to pray.

The dreams and stories and pieces of imagination, the wondering born at the edge of daybreak in the quiet of my room, were safe at my place at the table. My laughter, my different way of viewing the world, were welcome here. My place at the table was a place for my gifts. The invitation to partake of the feast and the invitation to be myself were the same thing. As an adult, as a parent, a teacher, a priest, a grown-up daughter and sister and partner and friend, when I am trying to understand what I can do or how I can be in a situation, it is to my place at the family table that I return—to know who I am, to rediscover my gifts, to understand what I can give.

The Lawrence table was a feast on any day, with its regular rhythms of setting the table, gathering around in our same places, holding hands as we sang in full harmony a hymn of thanks, and then breaking the bread. The legend in the community was that the Lawrences were always at table and that there was always, as the spiritual sings, *"plenty-good room,"* to sit down and break bread with us. One of my favorite times at home was when we were expecting company. Then it was time to go to the closet and get out the leaves for the dining room table. I loved the magic of opening the table, my sister on one end and me on the other, pulling straight and strong until we had a wide enough gap, matching up the notches, then closing the original table around it. This arrangement called for an extra large, special-occasion tablecloth to cover the faded leaf. I loved expanding our table, setting extra places, welcoming more people with their stories, their experiences, their gifts. I loved to bring my friends home to be a part of our family, and I loved to visit the families of my friends too. Their traditions and stories and family sayings, even the arguments that dared to flare up in the presence of company, enriched my life as ours from our table did theirs.

✹ ✹ ✹

"I will open my mouth in a parable; I will declare the mysteries of ancient times. That which we have heard and known, and what our forebears have told us, we will not hide from their children."[2]

My father, presiding from his end of the table, removes his glasses, poising one stem on the corner of his mustache. His ample eyebrows are raised, a sign of a parable coming forward from the pictures and sounds and feelings stored in his soul. As the telling unfolds, the picture I create in my imagination one of my Grandfather Charles, my father's father, listening to his father telling the parable to him.

Great-grandfather, Job Childs Lawrence, was the son of a Black slave and a white plantation owner. When his father ran short of funds because he had gambled his money away, Job was called to him and told that he and his mother would be sold to his father's brother. The father gave Job a silver dollar. Job Childs threw the silver dollar in the dirt and said I don't want your silver dollar and I don't want your name. And, so the legend goes, he turned and left and took the name Lawrence after people he knew and admired. And then the story ends with a refrain that was to be the refrain of many family stories to come: *He knew who he was and he was blessed.*[3]

When helpings had gone around many times ("Who's counting?" my mother always said), when the talking and eating had slowed to a full pace, my father, leaning back in his

---

2 Psalm 78:2,3

3 Adapted from a version of the legend retold to me by my mother, Margaret Lawrence and a version recorded by my sister, Sara Lawrence-Lightfoot in her biography of our mother, *Balm in Gilead, Journey of a Healer*, (New York, N.Y: Addison-Wesley) 1988

· · · · · ·

chair to admire the signs of appreciation for his irresistible cooking inventions, said, "Let's see now, what would you like to eat for supper?" It was a sign that this meal was over but never ending, only to be continued with an invitation to the next feast!

The gathering, the singing, the story telling, even the raising up of painful memories, but especially the breaking of bread, began at our family table and continued in the many gatherings, in all of their variety, around the Lord's Table of the churches of our lives. The invitation to the family table and the invitation to the Table on Sundays at church are inseparable for me. They are one invitation to Keep the Feast. And so I was raised to believe it would always be so. The life and strength and love would always be there in the breaking of the bread. *"I'm gonna sit at the welcome table one of these days, Hallelujah."*

"Can God set a table in the wilderness? God rained down manna upon them to eat and gave them grain from heaven. So they ate the bread of angels."[4]

It was at the family table that my parents first began to discuss plans for us to travel south as a family, to visit the family and friends where Mom and Dad had grown up. We had a brand-new 1954 Ford Country Sedan station wagon, dark green. In those days, there were no seat belts, and we rode with the back seats down. There were ridges along the floor, and my brother and sister and I had those ridges carefully divided by three. Because I was the youngest, I had the middle set of ridges and therefore two borders to guard over and no window. Chuck and Sara would sometimes let their stuff drift over into my section (on purpose, I was sure) and we'd get into a big, noisy argument. My father would simply pull the car to the side of the road and cut the engine off. We'd sit there in the long and awful silence

---

4 Psalm 78:19,24,25

well past the time when we'd gotten the point that the trip was not going to go on until we'd stop fussing. This was one of our traveling rituals.

Another of our rituals was stopping to eat our meals in restaurants. We'd sit down in the restaurant in the same pattern as we sat at home, told the same family jokes, rehearsed the same arguments, told the family stories. But when we got a little further south, about twenty miles beyond Philadelphia around Wilmington, Delaware, something different happened. There, my father, as always, pulled up to a restaurant, but this time he went in alone. He would come out looking atypically serious and get back in the car and quietly drive on. After this happened two or three times, my parents explained to us that this was a part of the country where brown-skinned people were not welcome to sit at table.

Now the picture I have of the table would forever include one in which all the people of one color, one economic status, one class, one religion, one section of town are seated for an elegant meal. And all of the people of different colors and languages and backgrounds are standing invisibly aside, silently waiting table. After they are done serving others, these people will eat dinner in the kitchen or just wait till they get back home.

I felt then a kind of hunger that comes to me still when I am in a place where it doesn't feel safe to be myself, where I have to unremember who I am in order to survive. And though it is a painful feeling, it is the seed of a food for fueling what would become my life's vocation—a vocation of breaking the Jim Crow rules about who gets to come to the table. It is a song that I will rehearse every day of my working life as a priest, a song whose lyrics are written in the words of poet and priest, Pauli Murray:

> When I consider how this frozen field
> Will hold within its harrowed breast
> A seed which shall in time
> Yield bread for hungering mouths,
>
> . . . . . .

> *I am at peace—*
> *Earth has her need of rain,*
> *And I of tears.*[5]

Now, as we are driving further on down the road, my brother and sister and I are huddled more closely—no real or imaginary borders between us. Just then, through the din of the newly started up motor and the sound of the tires on the road, I hear my father's voice calling me out of my wariness and fear, out of my loss of direction and loss of hope. He is speaking quietly but firmly the refrain from the stories of the family table: "We know who we are and whose we are, and we are blessed." Or is it Jesus saying, "Come and eat"?

Now I would forever and always hear the call to the Feast and know that God's summons is both invitation and demand—an invitation that demands of us that we acknowledge both our hunger for God and God's everlasting readiness to feed us. It is an invitation that calls us out of our brokenness into wholeness, out of whatever may be our segregated journeys into oneness as the children of God.

✳ ✳ ✳

"Afterwards, Jesus revealed himself to his students by the Delaware River, and this is how he revealed himself:"[6]

It is April third, 1986, the first day of my new job as principal of a school in Wilmington, Delaware. A few days earlier, in what would turn out to be our last telephone conversation, my dad, who has always been up on the details of my work life, counsels me about moving to Delaware, a state steeped in the ravages of segregation. He reminds me of the sorrow that

---

5 Pauli Murray. "Prelude to Spring" from *Dark Testament and Other Poems* (Norwalk, Connecticut, 1970) p.78

6 Paraphrase of John 21:1

erupted as violence in Wilmington the night Martin Luther King, Jr. was killed, and how Delaware's governor kept the National Guard there for nine and a half months—longer than any American city has been occupied by the military since the Civil War. But Dad is always the teacher, and so he gives me lots of room to learn this lesson my own way. My husband and I are aware of the racist, parochial, classist history here in this part of the country. John has commuted over two hours a day for fifteen years to his work in Delaware in order for us to raise our children in Pennsylvania, where our community celebrates their biracial being and where we, as adults, feel more connected personally and professionally to the changing world.

But Dad knows something about the resistant strain of the soil that we have yet to learn. Knowing how trusting his younger daughter has always been, knowing how persistent and tenacious ("stubborn," he calls me and says proudly that I was born that way), Dad tells me to be careful.

It is April third late at night. We are asleep in bed when the telephone rings. John answers then hands the phone to me. It is my mother calling to tell us that, having given his huge spirit to living, Dad's body has given way to death.

"We will go fishing,"[7] the disciples tell one another, looking for a way to proceed in life without their teacher. "I will go fishing," I say, trying like Peter and the others to find my way back through the aftermath of grief and loss to the feelings of former times. I am trusting, just as my dad knew I was. I trust that the soundest of religious and philosophical underpinnings of the school will support the charge I have been given as the first Black administrator in the 243-year history of the school to "make the school more diverse." I trust that, in that same context, I will be protected from the deep-seated racism practiced

---

7 Paraphrase of John 21:3

. . . . .

in the community beyond the school's pretty, green, manicured campus. It would be two years before I would learn that the suburban development in which the school resides had had, until recently, a strict all-white, all-Christian code in its civic association bylaws.

And so I spend the next three years ignoring the sometimes subtle but always persistent signs of racism that refuse to honor the boundaries of the school's doors. Daily I stand on the sidewalk outside of the school, opening car doors, welcoming each of nearly four hundred children and teachers by name, only to have some of the mothers, several weeks into the year, tell me without the slightest embarrassment that they are surprised that I am the principal and not the "help." "Teach, Paula. You are called to teach," and in so doing I prevail.

"We will go fishing," I tell myself each time a new offense flies in my face. But now and again my body feels the ache of bending over, the tedium of picking out of the empty nets traces of malice and wickedness. The occasional racist joke, the assumption made about a member of the community because of the color of his skin, the way she speaks, what neighborhood she or he comes from. Fragments of misunderstanding, splinters of being misunderstood, pieces of ignorance left over from the story one person tells about another in the absence of knowing their real story.

But the very stubbornness that is my gift keeps me fueled as I do what I can to make the school a place where children and their families are welcomed at the table, where they do not have to unremember who they are inside. And so season by season, moment by sometimes treacherous moment, we tell our stories. We bring them forward into the present tense where we live them together on the bus rides, in our talks together, as we settle arguments on the school yard, as we celebrate our lives together and break bread together at the school table. The words of comfort and explanation come when they are needed— not from me, but through me—from those who went before me and who go beside me.

They come from the family dinner table and car rides of my childhood, as my hair was brushed by my grandmother, as my mother and father sat at my bedside and gave me words that went through and beyond their own pain and anger and spoke simple prayers of healing and peace.

But all the while, those subtle but persistent fragments of racism picked from our nets and carelessly tossed back into the sea of daily life are infesting the very waters that would give us life. One day that stuff is bound to surface, and no one will ever know where that much hurt came from.

Then in my third spring, there is a traumatic racist incident at the school. On Mother's Day Monday morning, the phone rings in my office. It is the high school principal reporting that the kick board on the high school playing field has been painted with words and images of hatred. "Save the land, join the Klan," "Down with the Jews," and, worst of all, a bloody image of a Black student, recognizable by his car, with the inscription, "Kill the tar baby." It would soon be known that this was the work of four senior boys who had been students at the school since they were four years old.

In the horrendous days and weeks that follow, I notice for the first time, signs that, as the only person of color in the administration, I am not getting the support I need nor the acknowledgment of my pain that is a minimum requirement for stemming the tide of indignities flooding in from the community. And so the huge, blinding pain acknowledges itself.

At home, my husband and I watch our two high-school-age sons come and go, mostly silenced by their own confusion. John and I hold each other in our late-night exile, wondering how we can possibly remain. I can no longer hear my father's voice or the family story's encouraging refrain, "You know who you are, and you are blessed."

. . . . .

✳ ✳ ✳

"'Children, have you caught something to eat? Cast your net on the right side of the boat and you'll find something.' So they did, and they couldn't even drag the net anymore, what with the great mass of fish."[8]

Having nowhere else to go with my grief, I find myself at church saying plainly to the priest, "This Jesus who they say walks with me, does he stay out of this town because he knows better?" I am thinking about the tall, skinny, severe Sunday school teacher at St. Martin's in Harlem who flew around the table smacking us kids up-side the head if we forgot to bow on *"Jesus* loves me this I know." This is your Jesus? This is the kingdom of the Jesus that's supposed to be with us in all this hurt?

The priest and I sit still in the seething, grieving silence. After a while, he simply tells me the story of the Road to Emmaus. *Now on that same day, two of them were going to a village called Emmaus, about seven miles from Jerusalem, and talking with each other about all these things that had happened. While they were talking, Jesus himself came near and went with them, but their eyes were kept from recognizing him. And he said to them, "What are you discussing with each other while you walk along?" They stood still looking sad. Then one of them answered, "Are you the only stranger in Jerusalem who does not know the things that have taken place there in these days?" When they told him all that had happened, he said to them, "Oh how foolish you are and how slow of heart to believe all that the prophets have declared!" Then beginning with Moses and all the prophets, he interpreted to them the things about himself in all the scriptures.*

As they came near Emmaus, he walked ahead as if he were going on. But they urged him strongly saying, "Stay with us, because it is almost evening and the day is nearly over." So he went in to stay

---

8 John 21:5

with them. When he was at table with them, he took bread, blessed, and broke it, and gave it to them. Then their eyes were opened, and they recognized him; and he vanished from their sight. They said to each other, "Were not our hearts burning within us while he was talking to us on the road?"[9]

I am not sure why the priest is telling me this story, but remembering what I had learned to do as a little girl in times of confusion and pain, I begin to pray.

In the moments before daybreak a few days later I have a dream: *Our younger son, Abram, is driving the car, and I am in the front seat. His track bike is fastened to the roof rack. We are driving north into Pennsylvania on Route 100 early in the morning. There is a velodrome up there (a bowl-shaped bike track like the one they use in the Olympics) and Abe rides on it a couple of times a week. We are headed up there for an 8:00 a.m. training session. We are driving by a cornfield when I see my father standing by the side of the road. He looks healthy and slender and young, as he did when I was a little girl. This is not an extraordinary sight. He is not out of place or time. I say, "Abe, there's Grandpa. Pull over, let's see what's up." So Abe pulls the car over, and I turn down the window. Grandpa leans in and says, "I just want to know what you want to eat for supper tonight."*

I wake up and lie in bed long enough for the dream to dawn upon me. And when it does, I turn to my husband, John, who is sound asleep. "Where is Emmaus, Pennsylvania?" I ask him.

He answers me simply, as he always does whether asleep or awake, "It's up on Route 100 north of the velodrome."

The blinding loss of sadness and death is over. *"Come and eat,"* says the risen Lord.

---

9 Luke 24:13-27

. . . . .

70

6

Who will be a witness for my Lord?
Who will be a witness for my Lord?
Who will be a witness for my Lord?
My soul is a witness for my Lord.

BY THE TIME MY GRANDPARENTS came to live with us, the Rev. S. A. Morgan was presiding from his wheelchair. "Great day in the morning!" I can hear him say as he navigates his "chair" up the hallway and through the dining room door. "O My God!" he would cry out from behind closed doors, as he hoisted himself out of his chair with the still huge upper-body strength of his youth. "Confound it!" he'd grumble under his breath, cursing whatever obstacle was in his way. "Merciful Father," he'd complain on the out-breath of a deep and weary sigh as he rolled his wheelchair over the threshold of the door and onto the front porch.

In a recent telephone visit, I asked my mother why Grandfather's legs had been removed. In fifty-five years, I had never questioned this fact of life that we all lived with, nor asked to hear the full account, though bits of the story float around the edges of my consciousness like occasional cloudiness on the landscape of my memory. They are pieces I have heard but reject as too painful. Maybe not bringing it up is the remnant of my childhood offering of respect to my grandfather. When I was a child, my grandfather would from time to time complain that his feet hurt. Since he didn't have any feet that I had ever seen, mention of them was frightening fuel for my fertile imagination, and not something I would ever have pursued. But now, as Grandfather's litany of psalmist-like laments rises up into my consciousness anew, I find I want to know what I have refused to know until now.

On the weary out-breath of a sigh of her own, Mom begins to tell me about the arteriosclerosis that was the offending disease. She recounts her parents' trips to Nashville (where Mom was teaching at Meharry Medical School and where the hope was that there would be access to medical services superior to those of their home city of Vicksburg). She tells me of the efforts to save Grandfather's legs, remembering every detail of the house where we were living, how many steps there were from the dining room up to the alcove where my grandparents stayed, the little window in the alcove. "I can't recall how we got him back to Vicksburg after the surgery," Mom says, "We had the little Willys then." Then, conveying a deep admiration for her father's courage and faith, Mom adds, "What I do remember is that he never cried out in protest when his legs were to be removed. He never said, 'Don't do that.'"

When I tell my mother that I have been recalling his crying out aplenty, she laughs and says, "Oh, my father was not a saint! Neither of them was! He used to say to your grandmother, '*You* don't have to walk on *your* kidneys!'" Now we are both laughing. This is the grandfather I remember—the one who called stubborn people "bus-headed" and was proud to say that he knew one when he saw one!

But what my memory of Grandfather has mostly held intact all of these years is a feeling recalled in a picture. We are gathered on the sidewalk in front of the hedges of the house in Corona, Queens. Someone is taking our photograph. My sister stands on one side of Grandfather, my brother stands on the other. Grandfather says, "Paula, come stand over here in front of me, please, and be my legs." And so, at three years old, I stand as tall as I can. Grandfather's big, strong, priestly hands convey his unspoken gratitude to me as he holds me firmly by my shoulders.

When we moved to the country, Grandfather presided from his wheelchair at the top of our driveway, and if a neighbor passed down our road and paused for more than the tip of Grandfather's cap, the neighbor was in for one or two of his very lengthy stories. Most every story begins with the soon-to-be-broken promise, "I won't tell you the story about the time" and goes on and on with more than one broken promise of ending. "And so finally," Grandfather intones, and then goes right on with a new episode of the story he said he wasn't going to tell in the first place. As a little girl, I was interested but not amazed at the stories I heard him tell any willing listener about being the priest of St. Mary's Episcopal Church "Colored" in Vicksburg, Mississippi. He'd "get a feeling" that someone he knew was sick, and he'd follow that feeling down the road toward the person's house and offer that person, who would be waiting for him, healing.

When my mother, Margaret, was a little girl she was tough and adventurous and, the story goes, she went with Rev. Morgan when he went to visit the sick and lay his healing hands on them. She was allowed to carry the little basket with the silver set of miniature Communion things, a little basket I understood to be holy even as it sat through my growing-up years gathering dust on the pantry shelf. Years later I would understand what my child-heart already knew as I longed to play with the contents of that old, dusty basket. Years later, that little set of dishes would be significant props for my dreams and for the work God would call me to do in the world.

It is the summer of 1995, and I find myself facing a major season of reluctance in my spiritual journey. The summer before I have taken time away from the ecclesiastical drill of the ordination process to recover from major surgery and the resulting extended stay in the hospital. Now it is the summer when I have finally had to face my clinical pastoral education requirement. I have come to this intersection with determination, but with memories of both my recent sojourn in the hospital and the lengthy hospital stays of my childhood, long since rejected from the stories I tell anyone, including myself.

. . . . . .

I also return to this city just northeast of the Mason-Dixon line with a reluctance born of knowing that a mere two decades ago there were still "colored" and "white only" signs on water fountains and in movie theaters here. It is with this reluctance (and humility) that I am standing, as I have daily throughout the summer, at the door of Mrs. Sharon's room on the second floor of one of the city hospitals. The deep breath I draw in for courage pulls with it an ancient mix of hospital smells, transforming the reluctance not quite over the line into the physical sickness rising up from my knees into my stomach. A glance into Mrs. Sharon's room tells me that, once again, the second-floor nurses have left her lunch tray clear across the room where she can see it, but can't reach it. A beautiful, dark brown woman with silver eyes and silver hair, Mrs. Sharon has very little air in her very brittle lungs. Her gentle but persistent moans tell me that she has been trying to let someone on the staff know that she has been needing to use the bathroom for a long time. She and I have learned over her summer-long hospital stay (and mine) that if I inform the nursing staff that Mrs. Sharon needs the potty, they will dismiss both of us with "She's wearing a diaper. Don't worry about it." As I stand here, I am remembering again the beginning of the summer when the unit assignments were made. I had mentioned to the Pastoral Care Department secretary that I had been assigned to the second floor, and I couldn't miss the way she rolled her eyes and said with a note of cynicism, "Good luck!" I am remembering that I made a note to store that comment, but also not to make any assumptions about it.

But today, as every day, Mrs. Sharon's cry, though it is faint with her little bit of breath, is deeper and more penetrating than my reluctance. It calls to me through my own memories, both ancient and contemporary, to the strength of God in myself.

. . . . . .

"Here is my servant, whom I uphold, my chosen, in whom my soul delights; I have put my spirit upon her; she will bring forth justice to the nations.... . She will not grow faint or be crushed until she has established justice in the earth; and the coast lands wait for her teaching."[1]

The song of the servant, spoken in Mrs. Sharon's favorite psalms and sung in spirituals by her bedside, carries me across the threshold of reluctance each new day of the summer. Here, I help her put her teeth in, reach for her food on the days when she is up to eating, comb and brush her hair and let her wear her own nightgown. (The nurses daily hide it from us, but it is part of our sisterly conspiracy that we enjoy the triumph of daily finding it and getting it over her bony little shoulders.) Just when I think Mrs. Sharon has probably reached the limit of her energy, she settles her pretty head on her pillow and asks me to tell her how my work is going, how I'm doing on my journey to priesthood. Even as she asks me, the color in her cheeks returns, her breathing seems to get easier, and I hear in the tone of her questions echoes of my grandmother's voice from the back room, "Oooooo, Paulooooo. Is that you? Did you get your lessons today?"

The day before my last day at the hospital, I find myself in conversation with another patient, also an African-American woman, but in a room on the seventh floor. Despite a serious heart condition, this woman (who had once been for a time a chaplain in this hospital) is eager to have lots of conversation. Her habit of holding onto her audience by trailing one story into another is one not unfamiliar to me from my childhood. In fact, in many ways she reminds me of my grandfather. "I have something I want to ask you," I say, changing the subject but also in an earnest attempt to learn one particular story. "With all the history of

---

1 Paraphrase of Isaiah 42:1

segregation in this city as recently as the late sixties, how does the story of this hospital fit into that?"

There is a long pause before she tells me, "You see, back then, there were only five rooms in this hospital for colored. They actually had signs on the door of each of those rooms that said, 'colored.' There were no Black doctors allowed to practice here. And if you had six Black people sick, one of them was going to die in the hallway, that's for sure."

"Where were those rooms?" I ask, buying time to take in this not surprising but shocking story. "Oh, they were all down there on the second floor," she says. I am still trying to put the story together with the feelings I have been having all summer, with the sight of Mrs. Sharon's food too far to reach, and the sound of her crying out for dignity. "When did they take the signs down?" I ask mindlessly. "Oh," she says. "They're still up there. You just can't see them."

***

As a little girl I took notice of the fact that my grandmother had "bad spells" sometimes. As an adult, I would come to understand that she often gave in to huge bouts of depression; but as a child, I just thought of these as times when the world was too wounded for her, and maybe it was. But I also noticed that, whether it was helping me with my penmanship, teaching me to bake a cake from scratch, reminding me of my manners, or teaching me the Lord's Prayer down on her not-very-good knees by my bedside at night, Grandmother never had a "bad spell" when she was "helping me to get my lessons." It did not come as a total surprise to me when I became a teacher myself, and my mother told me that when Grandmother had school children "to see after," there were no bad spells. She was always up to the challenge.

"As soon as they left the synagogue, they entered the house of Simon and Andrew, with James and

John. Now Simon's mother-in-law was in bed with a fever, and they told Jesus about her at once. He came and took her by the hand and lifted her up. Then the fever left her, and she began to serve them."[2]

In the passages which precede this story of Jesus' healing ministry, the writer of Mark tells us of Jesus' building up of the kingdom, literally edifying through his teaching and healing in the synagogue. Now he takes what at first glance seems to be an elective detour to another part of town to heal this minor character known only by her in-law relationship to one of his disciples. But as I read the story aloud, in the way my grandmother taught me "to get my lessons," I hear the meaning crystallize around the words, *"Then the fever left her, and she began to serve them."* I hear these words, and I see my grandfather, not in his wheelchair, but standing tall in his clerical clothes, striding down the Mississippi road with his brown-skinned daughter, her plaits bouncing down beyond her shoulders on her back as she moves her strong, young legs to keep up with him. She has a little basket of healing dishes in her hands. I hear these words, and I hear my grandmother's voice calling me from the back room where she has undoubtedly spent the day with another "bad spell." But now that her grandchildren are home from school, it is time to see that we "get our lessons." I know that soon I will see her emerge from her "fever" and begin to "serve." I hear, *"Then the fever left her, and she began to serve them,"* and I am reminded of what I understood as I grew up in a household where healing was a way of life, a way of living as we answer the call to "continue the work God wants done."[3]

I leave the seventh floor and go directly to see Mrs. Sharon, more than ever dreading my visit to the second floor, more than ever reluctant, as I will have to tell Mrs. Sharon that tomorrow will be my last visit. I decide to explain to her that it is because I must go back

2 Mark 1:29-31

3 Joan Chittister. *Wisdom Distilled from the Daily, Living the Rule of St. Benedict Today* (San Francisco, CA.: Harper and Row, 1990)p.86

. . . . . .

to school. I'm hoping she will understand my needing to get on with my education. Mrs. Sharon makes no comment, but puts her head back on the pillow and says, "Will you sing today?" "Sure," I say, relieved that she isn't complaining or asking for further explanation. "What do you want me to sing?" *"Angels watching over me,"* she says, and closes her eyes as she always does to listen.

"All night, all day, Angels watching over me, my Lord…" I begin, but suddenly I am in the grip of sadness and the lump in my throat is closing off the sound. The hospital sounds and smells flood into the silence left over as my voice trails off. Suddenly I hear a full, beautiful, spirited soprano voice picking up the song where I left off. *"If I could I surely would, stand on the rock where Moses stood."* It is Mrs. Sharon. She is sitting up and singing. *"Then the fever left her, and she began to serve them."*

On the last day, I go back three times to try to say good-bye to Mrs. Sharon, but she is sound asleep, her head peaceful and pretty on the pillow, her hairbrush and pins neatly placed on her bed stand. At home that night, I tell John, my husband, that I'm going to need to go back in the morning because I haven't had a chance to say good-bye to Mrs. Sharon. He says quietly, "I think Mrs. Sharon may be crossing the bridge now that she's seen you off to school." When I get to the second floor the next day, Mrs. Sharon's hospital bed is empty. The nurses inform me gently that she died peacefully in her sleep just after I left the evening before.

I leave the hospital in the warm, peaceful, healing glow of the Saturday morning sunshine. I decide to walk along the river a little ways in the park below the hospital before I get back in my car and get on with an ordinary day. I'm thinking maybe I'll actually see Mrs. Sharon crossing one of those bridges over the water, and I'll wave just one more time.

Instead I see Grandfather in a dream I had years ago, when I first knew I was called to be a priest. The little healing dishes carried by his daughter on their way to answer the call are in the dream too.

In the daytime reality before the dream, it is Easter of 1977. I have telephoned my parents to tell them of the invitation to be one of the first two female chalice bearers at Trinity Church in Swarthmore, Pennsylvania, where we live. My parents send me a hooded alb with a cincture. The night before my first Sunday at the altar, I try on the alb. A feeling of warmth moves high in my chest. I know this is right, but I am anxious. It is new and not new all at once. Naturally, some pieces of my imagination and history work themselves into the dream's images: Trinity Church has two chalices. One is slender and smaller; the other is broader and somewhat top-heavy. I think of them as feminine and masculine and, though I tell no one, I have secretly named the chalices after our male and female cats, Moses and Fidelity. And the history: When I was a little girl, my grandfather spoke about wishing he could have worn the "big sleeves" (wishing he could have become a bishop).

Moments before Easter dawns, a dream visits me in the clarity of full color and sound: *I am standing at the Communion rail, wearing my white alb. I am preparing stuff, setting the table. The door to the chancel creaks open. I am thinking that my grandfather used to say that when a door opens without explanation, it is the Holy Spirit coming through. Something new is going to happen. Something is about to change. Just then, I look up and Grandfather is standing at the door. He stands tall and proud in his clerical garb. He has the big sleeves. He is holding the Moses and Fidelity chalices in his hands. I put down the things I am getting ready and turn to him. He says in a deep, serious voice, "Well, we couldn't have done this in my time, but I suppose it is okay now."*

***

"The stone that the builders rejected has become the chief cornerstone. This is the Lord's doing; it is marvelous in our eyes."[4]

In my seminary days, I regularly presided at the Service of the Word at a 9:00 a.m. inter-generational folk Eucharist. Some sixty to eighty people showed up every Sunday. A gloriously motley crowd we were—mothers, children, fathers, college students, grandparents by themselves, grandparents with grandchildren. One family regularly came with four children, including one who was eight years old and confined to a wheelchair with a scaffold of braces and straps to keep him erect. Reed, a tender and expressive child, liked his wheelchair to be parked right in the crossing of the sanctuary, right in the midst of the goings on. So I was always standing beside Reed as I began the service with a request that the congregation "please stand."

One Sunday, as I was about to begin, Reed's eyes met mine, and I could suddenly say nothing at all. I was suddenly struck with a picture of Reed at my age responding with resentment when somebody asked him why he had stopped going to church, or why he hated being there. A by-then fifty-one-year-old Reed would say, "When I was a child I used to love to go to church. But there was this woman who would stand there every Sunday and tell us to stand up, and I couldn't stand up. So I just stopped going."

Well, there I stood beside eight-year-old Reed with the threads of my own intentions for an inclusive liturgy lying bare and unraveled on the sanctuary floor. I don't remember what I might have said next; but after the service, I found Reed's parents and asked to have a private word with them. When I told them what my worry was, Reed's mother's eyes filled

---

4 Psalm 118: 22,23

. . . . . .

with tears, and she said, "I'm crying not because you asked, but because you are asking." Then, in the rabbinical tradition of Jesus himself, she answered my question with a question of her own: "What is it that you want when you ask him to stand?"

The answer to Reed's mother's tender question came to me, not in words at first, but in a picture, a picture of myself at Reed's age. In the picture I am eight years old and in the hospital in New York. As the result of very difficult and long emergency surgery, I am paralyzed. I can't walk and I can't eat. Legions of doctors, residents, nurses, and technicians have prodded and poked and x-rayed. I am attached everywhere to tubes and machines of mysterious origin. A person of both sweet and stubborn temperament, I smile through the discouragement with their own efforts that I can read on the doctors' faces.

My mother, a physician herself, keeps nothing hidden from me. She explains carefully what is happening. Still, I know by her careful words that the medical staff has run out of things to try. But my mother is more mother than physician. *"Why do you make a commotion and weep?"*[5] she says with her eyes and her body and her determination to believe. And moving the doctors aside, my mother props me up—i.v. poles, straps, braces and all and says, "Paula Jean, walk!" *"Talitha cum."* "Little girl, arise."[6] And immediately I am walking, one trying, stumbling, miraculous step at a time. My mother tells the doctors through the tears of joy streaming down her face, *"Get her something to eat."*[7]

"What is it that you want when you ask him to stand?" Reed's mother had asked me just moments before, and now, having been brought back in Reed's presence to my own story

---

5 Mark 5:39

6 Mark 5:41

7 Mark 5:43

I hear the refrain of Jesus' words to Jairus' daughter: "Little girl, get up—arise."

"He is risen," I say aloud to Reed's parents. "I want us to arise in the spirit of the risen Lord."

"Maybe you could say that," says Reed's mother.

On the following Sunday, I begin the service where I always have, at the crossing by Reed's side. "Let us rise in the spirit of our risen Lord," I say. And Reed, right beside me, nearly flies up into my arms. The rest of the congregation rises with such energy, that its collective feet barely touch the ground, and the singing is fuller than I have ever heard it in this place. Reed grew and became strong, filled with wisdom, and the favor of God was upon him. And we were filled with wisdom, and the favor of God was upon us, too.

7

Walk together children, don't you get weary.
Walk together children, don't you get weary.
Walk together children, don't you get weary.
There's a great camp meeting in the promise land.

You shall have the trumpet sounded throughout the land. And you shall hallow the fiftieth year and you shall proclaim liberty throughout the land to all its inhabitants. It shall be a jubilee for you: you shall return, every one of you, to your property and every one of you to your family...you shall not sow, or reap the aftergrowth, or harvest the unpruned vines. For it is a jubilee; it shall be holy to you: you shall eat only what the field itself produces.[1]

Longer, colder nights are upon us. Earth clothes her northern parts in the cover of darkness as she orbits toward the winter solstice. Here, as she rests in the long turn of the night, she recalls once again the holy darkness before the dawn of her first light. And so it is with me in these last weeks of my jubilee year, that I pause in the darkness before the dawn of my fiftieth birthday. Here in the holy darkness, I am turned toward the essence of the gift of God within me, toward the work I am called to do in this world. Here in the quiet, I am turned toward home.

It is June, 1995. My mother has joined me in San Francisco where I am to preach a sermon at Grace Cathedral as part of the year-long celebration of the United Nations Jubilee Year, and the fiftieth anniversary of the signing of the United Nations Charter. We have arrived a day early to walk the labyrinth. We have been anticipating for months this first walk

---

1 Leviticus 25

for each of us on the ancient path, and we plan to walk it in celebration of our jubilee year as mother and daughter.

It is late Saturday morning, and after a good, long visit over breakfast, we hike up the hill with fresh enthusiasm. We find the cathedral door open and welcoming. But instead of the quiet, meditative environment where we hope to find our center, the cathedral is filled with the familiar noises and smells and not a little chaos emitting from what seems to be the annual diocesan acolyte festival. A bishop is telling the story of how he first came to be a thurifer (as a child, he was good with a yo-yo). At first, Mom and I pay attention as we have been taught to do in church. But since the labyrinth is not available for walking right now (and anyway, since we know how the story turns out—people who are good with yo-yos have a good chance of becoming bishops), we turn and leave the cathedral and head out into the city to find a bite to eat.

Walking to the restaurant is a breeze. Mom and I, as always, are talking as we walk, and we fail to notice the negative incline of our path. After lunch, as we make our way back toward the cathedral to walk the labyrinth, the San Francisco hills make themselves fully known to us. "Don't you think the other side of the street looks a little less steep?" asks my mother, slightly breathless, but ever the optimist. And so we cross over and climb on that side for a while. Several zig-zags later, we are mounting one last hill and pausing to grab our collective breath when my mother cries out, "What if I find my center before I get there!" The side-splitting laughter that follows is new fuel for our journey, propelling us onward and upward toward our destination.

At last we are in the nave of the cathedral, walking barefoot on the ancient path. We walk in silence with a respectful distance between us. As the path takes me on the circuitous route through the twists and turns, weight by weight is lifted first from my chest and shoulders,

. . . . . .

then from my mind and my heart. Soon gravity's residue from my life is scattered in dribs and drabs behind me on the cathedral floor.

✷ ✷ ✷

A few months later, I have returned with a friend to walk the newly created labyrinth in the cathedral garden. This time, it is the experience of the turns themselves, the experience of being turned and returned, that is so powerful. As I come out of each turn in a new direction, I hear a message which in its clarity as well as its content echoes the Hebrew Scripture's charge for the jubilee year: *Discipline, Paula. Discipline yourself. Take only what you need, lighten your load for God's work ahead.* In the turns in the path I am led to listen more and say less, to be more economical than my temperament would otherwise lead me to be. I hear the voice of a friend who is an extraordinary artist and educator. He is speaking to his students about their compositions. "What you have going for you is negative space," he tells them. Now the labyrinth speaks to me in his gentle voice: The retreats, the silence, the dark are as important as the light, the waiting as essential as the creating, the rests as nourishing as the musical notes.

The message of the labyrinth follows me back across the country, up the Amtrak line, through the doors opening onto the seminary close, and up four flights of well-worn stairs to my room. Up at the crack of dawn, as I am trying to put dent by dent in the pile of sermons, papers, exams, proposals for next semester, I discover I can still feel the turning of the labyrinth walk. Fueled in the turns themselves, I am aware of being directed through the seemingly overwhelming volume of stuff to do. Discipline. Simplicity. Lighten your load. Be selective. Travel lightly. Step by progressive step, I am moving beyond myself, breaking through the bonds of what I had always thought was the only way I could approach a problem, breaking through to an experience of my unseen self, the gift of God within me. I am being turned—toward something—something at the heart of the matter. And then in the dark, in the silence, in the "negative space," a moment of grace, the experience of peace. As I drift off to sleep, I am remembering what I was taught in Hebrew class about the multiplicity and yet oneness of the meanings of the word *torah*: rule, instruction, law, revelation, light. This path of discipline leads to the apple of God's eye!

✳ ✳ ✳

It is Saturday morning. The purple and amber light barely poking between the dark tree branches has awakened me. Stuart, our loving golden dog, is already awake, having heard an angel's voice still out of human hearing. He pads down the carpeted steps in the still dark house and waits with wagging tail by the back door for the appearance of his friend whose voice he hears.

And now, as I struggle to pull on my jeans and tug my sweatshirt over my sleepy head, as I tip down the stairs in sock feet, my walking shoes in tow, I too hear the angel voice, as full and clear as if it were noonday. "*God is love, and love enfolds us,*" she sings. "*All the world in one embrace….*" She is already on the second verse, or maybe she has come around to it a second or third time somewhere between their house and ours. Stuart pads back up the stairs to get me in case I haven't heard. "Toni is here," he says with his eyes and his tail and his tongue and his breath and his ample wiggle. "Toni is here! Let her in! Let her in!"

And so I do, sleepy and sock-footed as I am. She and Stuart are in the kitchen making mischief with Moses the cat while I, sitting on the hallway steps, pull on my walking shoes. The singing has subsided to a gentle hum when suddenly Toni's laughter splits the early morning quiet of the house. I know by this particular laugh that Toni and her canine co-conspirator are up to no good. My suspicions are confirmed as I come around the corner into the kitchen in time to see that Toni has put her purple earmuffs on our golden retriever. All three cats have a look of disgust on their faces. They don't see the humor in it. "Let's get out of here," I say, "before we wake up the whole neighborhood." But we have no real intentions of being quiet as we set out with fierce pace against the cold morning air.

We are walking off our exhaustion. We are walking off our burdens. We are scheming against our frustrations. We are shedding our mistakes. We are puzzling at things we don't understand. We are railing against being misunderstood. We dare to ask questions we know have no answers—no ignorance too great to march out into the light of this glorious day. We are walking off our grief, our pain, our fury, our outrage at a wounding, sometimes unjust, occasionally downright ugly world.

And just then, from somewhere down deep within us, from some place where we are connected by a past that walked generations before this walk began, from a place far in front of us that knows hope we can't know in the present tense of ourselves, comes a moment of schoolgirl silliness. We are bumping be-hinds like nine-year-olds on the recess yard, hooting wildly as we do imitations of our teachers, facing off to each other with our hands on our hips. "Just who do you think you are, Missy?" says Toni up in my face. And we are doubled over in raucous rebellion against anybody who ever did anybody else any hurt or wrong— even ourselves. We were raised, we were, among people who know strength that comes out of struggle and humor as a form of grace. "Good thing we don't bitter!" I say as we wipe laughter's tears from our cheeks.

Stuart has circled back around to check out whatever the laughter is about. He's laughing too, but now it's time to get on with the walk. We are walking in our former rhythm now, back to the crisp pace of the walk's beginning as we round the last corner. "Please, God," Toni shouts out to a sky that is no longer purple and amber but later-morning blue.

· · · · · ·

"Give me a sign, God. Talk to me, God. Pray with me." And as though she never stopped singing in the first place, Toni picks up the hymn where she left off.

This time, a few neighbors, retrieving their papers from the bushes at the end of their driveways, look first curiously at the sight of this motley, colorful threesome walking boisterously through their tidy streets. But they smile in spite of themselves when they hear the angel's voice lifted in song: *"And when human hearts are breaking under sorrow's iron rod, then we find that self-same aching deep within the heart of God."*

Toni is here! Let her in! Let her in!

* * *

It is the fall of 1995. Even as I am learning to follow this circuitous path, I am constantly overwhelmed by the treachery of things in my sight but out of my reach. The verdict of the infamous murder trial in Los Angeles this fall has been hard on every person, institution, and community I know of. Treacherous emotions are coursing through my veins and through the blood and guts of the entire nation as we hear and absorb the astonishing news. This complex and traumatic event has deleted everything we thought we knew (or as a country pretended we knew) about race relations, domestic relations, interracial relations, the justice system, children's advocacy, professional athletics, and responsible journalism. The ugly events of the last few days have unearthed irreversible injury carved deep in the historical memory of African-American people, passed down through generations, going back to a time of arriving on the shores of this nation, not hopeful, but enslaved. Now a fracture infinitely bigger than the San Andreas fault running deep beneath the City of Angels' streets, a fracture that has lived as a silent but festering wound in the heart of this country for a few hundred years, has erupted with violence and confusion.

It is October fourth, Yom Kippur, the day after the country stood still for a few minutes to hear the verdict announced. I am sitting in the seminary chapel, an endless flow of hot, molten tears leaking out of the fracture in my heart. I know from almost fifty years of dragging my wounds to church, that this is a place where I can nourish my doubts, let them sink to their full depths and rise to their full, cumbersome, homely heights. I am down on my knees in this place of refuge and strength asking God to help me understand, when I hear the lector reading the words of St. Paul to the people of Corinth. "If one member of the body suffers, all suffer together with it." My mind flashes angrily to the late-night news. Why, when parts of the body have been living with the cancer of racism for so long, is everyone so surprised that it has spread to the whole body? And will we be equally surprised as the evils of homophobia, sexism, anti-Semitism, classism, ageism, xenophobia and countless other injuries, seen and unseen, fully reveal themselves after living silently as part of the body all along?

I am still down on my knees, lost in turbulent images of imminent terror, by now of my own making, when I look up and see the preacher gesturing toward the cross. He is telling us that the cross beckons us to remember, and then with the gift of God's grace, to hope.

So this is it for me. The path has led me to this place where there is a glimpse of hope. It has led me to the apple of God's eye where, in God's presence, I hear echoes of the Jubilee call: *You shall proclaim liberty throughout the land to all its inhabitants.* And so I know anew that it is here in the holy darkness, even in the treachery of this world—or because of it—that I am turned toward the essence of the gift of God within me, toward the work I am called to do in this world.

✳ ✳ ✳

This Jubilee time of turning and return finds me at peace with the dark and the silence, and, for the time being, turned toward home. Here John and I land wearily at the end of our long days. We walk and talk—first about the nonsense of our work, the challenges big and small, engaging and tedious. As the path takes us on the circuitous route through the twists and turns toward the shared center of our relationship, weight by weight is lifted first from our shoulders then from our minds and hearts. For the time being, gravity's residue from our life is scattered in dribs and drabs on the road behind us.

By the time we land at home, we have landed on a shared longing that connects the story of the ancient fossils of the coastal islands off of the low country of South Carolina and the stories, ancient and new, told in God's time. We are connected, as we have been from the beginning, by our reverence for all that is deeper and broader than ordinary time can measure.

Then, in a moment of grace given to us in unmeasured time, we light the candles over a simple supper, and say a word of thanks for the spirit of God's steadfast love shown to us in the children of every age and color that God puts in our lives to love us and know us, to cheer us on and smother us in affection. Like the earth resting in the turn of the night, we pause momentarily in the dark before being turned in our course. We celebrate simply the simple blessings of our lives and we talk tenderly about next things.

8

Gonna put on my long white robe
Down by the riverside, down by the riverside, down by the riverside.
Gonna put on my long white robe
Down by the riverside
And study war no more.

We are in a line dance—brothers and sisters, mothers and fathers, children of every color and race from all over the world. We are dressed in flowing white robes, moving in a dance as if one body, energy stirring from one white-robed dancer to another. Now and then one dancer moves away from the line, setting off waves in a new direction. Arms flung wide, heads high then low then high, our hands are open to the sky. The dance comes toward us and from us and through us all at once. Now we are climbing a mountain and now moving through the desert, our long, twisting collective shadow rippling on the red, hot sand beneath our feet.

As we cross whole continents and generations and centuries, new daughters and sons join the line making their own rhythms and forms and stories a part of our dance. Soon we come to the edge of a great sea, the waves lapping loudly toward us. We dance back at the sea, echoing its thunder and roll. All at once the waves in our line echo with such resonance and force that there is lift. Our feet no longer touch the earth or the water. Our white-robed sleeves are transformed into wings and we are weightless and free, soaring all over God's heaven!

It is a recurring dream from my childhood, and like the spirituals whose refrains run through it, the dream's story brings forth something from the memory residing in my soul and in the souls of generations who went before me. The jubilant sounds of the spirituals' refrains hold the promise of something I cannot see in the present reality, but I feel

· · · · · ·

the possibility of its promise with all my being. It is the promise of reconciliation, of beauty, of energy, wholeness, love and freedom. It is the promise of shalom.

It is Saturday afternoon of Holy Week. Late winter in the Northeast does not even hint at the coming of Easter. It seems as though Lent will last forever. I drag my weary feet to the church where I am expecting to meet two little girls to rehearse their dance for the Easter Vigil—the story of the parting of the Red Sea. One of the girls has her cousin in tow—"Can she be in it?" she asks, "Three is a better number anyway!"—and a few minutes of loaves-and-fishes magic later, there is enough purple and teal and magenta fabric to make two costumes into three.

We sit cross-legged on the floor at the crossing of the church's empty nave, their fierce giggling finally subsiding now as I begin to tell them the story of Moses leading the Israelites across the Red Sea. As soon as I begin to sing the Hebrew tune—*torah orah, torah orah*—and beat the sweet spot on my drum, they are up on their feet. "We could do this," one says, raising her arms up high. "Yeah," says the next, "like the priest does when we are going to have the bread." "Let's stretch out our arms to be the waves," says the third. They can hardly catch enough breath to say it. They are already the waves, heads high then low then high. "Then I'll dance on through you," says the first, and she has just cartwheeled up the aisle. The other two follow with their own variations, setting off waves of energy in new directions. "Now we'll dance around the Baptism Fountain!" they are saying in unison, and they have joined hands, a twirling circle around the pool of water.

There seem to be more than three dancers and yet only one, spirit and energy and life coming through them. Woven into the memory of the fabric of their souls is this ancient story of God's saving deeds. As it is brought forth now through their bodies and imagined in new ways by these child dancers, the waves in their line echo with such resonance and

· · · · · ·

force that all at once there is lift. Is it the echo of a recurring dream or are they really here now, soaring weightless and free all over God's heaven?

When the rehearsal is over, I turn and, out of habit, dip my hand in the baptismal font. With the little bit of new and yet ancient water, I make the sign of the cross on my brow. As the children line up solemnly behind me and take turns dipping and signing, I feel a refreshing wave of remembrance come from somewhere deep within me. It is a feeling I have come to know as the everlasting child in each one of us. "Thank you for teaching us the dance," says one. "Oh no, I didn't teach you, you taught me," I say. "Well," she says, "thank you for making it available to us so we could be the rememberers!"

"Take off the garment of your sorrow and affliction, O Jerusalem, and put on forever the beauty of the glory of God. Put on the robe of the righteousness that comes from God."[1]

I am thirteen years old, back in the room of my growing-up house, getting ready to go out somewhere with my friends. I have changed my outfit no fewer than nine times. I know, even as I take the first item off, that I will change my mind many more times over, heaving the outfits of my frustration and ambivalence, one by one on the bed, on the floor, over the door knob, wherever. It is a hopeless search, and I know it because it is not about how the clothes look from the outside, but how I feel on the inside. To say, at thirteen, it feels awkward is to give it the benefit of extreme understatement. Each item of clothing seems to hang on a weird curve or a newly formed angle, betraying my wildly unfinished self. When I finally emerge from my room, my dad is encouraging about the final image, even as he comments on the mess I've left behind in my wake. "How," he asks rhetorically, "does a pretty girl like you come out of a *hoorah's* nest like that?" I don't know exactly what a hoorah

---

1 Baruch 5: 1-2

is or how she might have felt beneath her plumage when she finally emerged from her nest, but I know that for me, the transformation is definitely incomplete.

After more than three decades of marriage, my husband can tell by my footsteps upstairs and the opening and closing of the closet door, when I'm having a "bad clothes day," as we call it. And though for the most part I pick up after myself now, I still have times when the way I feel about going somewhere (something hard I have to face, something I don't feel too confident about) will make the clothes hang on my body just as awkwardly as they did when I was thirteen. "It's a good thing you suit up in that white robe to go to church," John tells me, knowing how many hills and valleys and crooked roads of ambivalence and frustration and fear lie between me and the call I must answer in that beloved place!

But friends and strangers alike know that, more often than not, the garment I end up putting on is woven in bright purples and gold, turquoise, reds, magentas and oranges. "A coat of many colors," is often the comment people make, intending a compliment, I think. "Thank you," I say out loud, even as I am thinking what a high price Joseph paid for the coat they are alluding to, the coat of many colors that caused him to be heaped in hate and resentment and betrayal by his own brothers. Later Joseph would say, "*Even though you intended to do harm to me, God intended it for good*."[2] But still I wonder, did he remember mostly the love in the coat, or was it for him a coat of sorrow?

✳ ✳ ✳

It is winter in the last of my college years. I am sitting at a tiny desk in my dormitory room. A large poster of Judith Jamison, principal dancer of the Alvin Ailey American Dance Theater, figures prominently on the wall above my head. When I am at my lowest or most

2 Genesis 50:20

alone or most filled with fear, which I sometimes am in these college years, Judith Jamison herself very nearly dances out of that poster and into my room, her head held high, arms outstretched, quiet and powerful in her flight overhead. Her smooth, dark brown skin is clothed in a sparkling white dress, fitted to her strong, lean body at the top, a swirling skirt moving with the wind beneath what seem to be wings. The dance is called *"Cry,"* and as I peer up from my own small glumness and inertia of will at her grace-filled ascent, sudden and surprising tears fill my eyes. But these are tears of joy. Her weightless flight through my dormitory room comes as a reminder to me to lay my burdens down.

Twenty-three years later, I am living with my family twenty-three minutes down the highway from my college dormitory in the suburbs outside a city that is still, in the late eighties, steeped in the ravages of segregation. We have moved here to be closer to our work and our sons' school, but the subtle but persistent signs of racism have warred at us with a relentlessness that will no longer be ignored. A traumatic racist incident at the school has sent us, and many others we don't even know, into hundreds of little, private exiles. We sing no songs of joy here by the waters of suburban Babylon as we stand discouraged and fearful and less than ambivalent at the doors of closets filled with robes of sorrow.

Judith Jamison is no longer regularly dancing, but is now artistic director of her own company which has come to perform at the Grand Opera House. I reluctantly accept the invitation of a high school friend of our son to attend this concert which she tells me will be a chance of a lifetime. "Whose lifetime?" I am thinking as I drag my feet to the concert hall beside my young, optimistic companion. Even as I sit and watch this strong and engaging performance high up and away from some of the establishment of the city, the citizens uncomfortable with the beautiful coat of color I was born with, the weight of worry and fear and sadness sits heavy on my heart.

At the end of the evening, in a final piece, the whole company appears on stage in a kind of line dance. They are dressed in flowing white robes. They are moving as if one body, energy stirring from one white-robed dancer to another. They are dancing my recurring dream! And now it is Jamison herself, her arms flung wide, hands open, head high then low then high. She reaches up and out and up to me. I am on my feet. She is flying toward me, the skirts of her full white robe embracing me, folding gently around me. And now, way up here in the balcony, I am weightless, I am triumphant, I am free.

At home again, I sit at the late-night dining room table savoring the evening, going through the program booklet again and again. For the first time, now, I see that the last piece is called *Read Matthew 11:28*. Must be the Bible, I say out loud to no one in particular. I bound up the stairs to my study to retrieve my Bible. There in the twenty-eighth verse is the white-robed dance all over again: *"Come unto me all you that are weary and carry heavy burdens, and I will give you rest. Take my yoke upon you, and learn from me; for I am gentle and humble in heart, and you will find rest for your souls. For my yoke is easy and my burden is light."*[3]

✴ ✴ ✴

"Gonna lay down my burdens, down by the riverside, and study war no more."

In the early weeks or months of 1992 when I had recently celebrated my forty-sixth birthday, a dream visited either in the daylight hours or at night, I can't remember which. I only recall the strong images in the dream and their teachings.

I am standing on a wooded path at the opening in an old stone wall. An old wooden trail marker is nailed to a tree beside the path. On the sign, numbers are written in chalk in the form of a fraction: "46/92." There is nothing out of the ordinary about this marker. I know how to read trail markers, and its intention is immediately obvious to me. It is marking the half-way point of my life. (I was born

---

3 Matthew 11:28

in 1946 and I have just turned 46 years old.) Now I recognize the chalked letters as the handwriting of Mr. Leo Valentine Dustman, my high school geometry teacher named for the holiday on which he was born. I see myself at the dining room table of my growing-up years, imitating Mr. Dustman doing proofs: "Let's say you have lived 46 years of stories and you have 46 more years," he is saying. "Do you think you can carry all these stories with you?" I put down a big heavy old satchel I did not even know I'd been carrying. It is full of stones. I begin to sort through it, removing the stones one at a time, examining each one and remembering its story. It is suddenly clear to me that there are some stones I can't possibly afford to take with me into the second half.

My dreams, both day and night, have been my teachers. I know from this dream that I must decide which stories will come with me to the second half of my life and which must be left here beside the road. As I look through the contents of that satchel, I come across some broken, old stories that I know have been nourished with too much attention and too many tellings. I see, now, as I turn each stone over in my hands, how more tellings have not improved them. Rather, telling them again and again only seems to add weight to my load.

Not long after that dream had visited me, I led a spiritual retreat with a group of educators. I brought a huge basket of stones with me, stones my geologist husband and I have collected on field trips and adventures throughout the years. At the beginning of the retreat, I placed the basket of stones on the altar, and I invited the participants to choose a stone to represent the resentments and grudges they were currently holding, and to carry that stone with them throughout the three-day retreat. I told them they'd be carrying the stones while they eat, sleep, shower, walk in the woods, even while they pray. Eagerly, they chose stones— heavy ones, ugly ones, motley ones—metaphors for the burdens in their lives. Some of them were greedy enough to choose two or three stones to represent their resentments and frustrations. By the second day, most of them were exhausted from the chore of carrying these weights around.

. . . . . .

At our afternoon meditation on the second day, I read them a single phrase, the words of the father of Martin Luther King, Jr., "Daddy King." He said, "Don't hate, it's too big a burden to bear."[4] One by one over the next few days, the stone carriers returned their stones to the altar.

I stand on the wooded path at the opening to the second half of my life, and I choose the stories that will go with me. They are the stories that are still teaching, the stories that are still healing in the telling. The stories that I choose to take on the journey are the ones whose resounding refrains will echo who I am as a child of God.

✳ ✳ ✳

"I will pour living water upon you. A new heart I will give you, and a new spirit I will put within you; and I will take out of your flesh the heart of stone and give you a heart of flesh. And I will put my spirit within you."[5]

It is July of 1981. John and our sons, Wes and Abram, and I have come across the country to Canyon de Chelly in Arizona. We arrive for our hike into the canyon on a day when, atypically, it is pouring rain, a sudden, prolonged and heavy rainstorm. We are huddled in our raincoats at the rim of the canyon when John begins to tell us this story:

Two hundred million years ago, red sand accumulated in mountain-size, desert-like sand dunes. Sand accumulated layer upon layer, sloping on the down-wind side. Tens of thousands of years later, the forms of the original sand dunes are preserved in beautiful rock. Water that falls on the landscape will flow, he tells us, *if it has a slope. If it is flowing, it has the power to change the land. Given enough time* (and when we ask him how much time, he tells us a short time—five to ten million

---

4 MLK Sr. quote from Sheron C. Patterson's *I Want to Be Ready* (Nashville, TN.: Abingdon Press) p.27

5 Ezekiel 36: 25,26

years) *the water develops into a channel that is the river of today. All the while the water is flowing, it is carving sediment and removing it to the delta where the river meets the sea. Meanwhile, forces of uplift are moving the surface of the earth up and down, building mountains, creating the slope down which the river flows. What you see today,* he tells us, *is the balance between uplift and erosion—two competing forces— the balance between mountain building and the river flowing.*

We know that most of the time here in this part of the country, there is no rain. Only we, the visiting easterners, have raincoats to put on. When there is a thunderstorm, sudden, violent, and powerful water runs rapidly down the steep, impervious sandstone cliffs into the riverbed, creating a flash flood. And now, first to our ears as a rumbling, and then to our eyes, the white water at the head of a brown, noisy river, rises in the riverbed down below.

When the storm subsides, the river subsides, and we follow the steep trail down into the wet-walled canyon. It is deeply quiet and we make no noise of our own. We take off our shoes to cross the muddy wash of the riverbed. A Navajo woman herding sheep back from the watering hole is crossing too at a distance, and the bahs and bells of her sheep echo against the wet walls. We look up at the walls to see where the echo has come from, and are struck by how the rain has deepened the colors of the walls, purples and reds now emerging.

The rushing flood waters come through us and change us as, in the fullness of God's time, the waters have come through and changed this canyon. But it is the deep, wet, purple quiet at the center of it all which has become part of us and calls us back home to a feeling of peace. "If the water is flowing, it will have the power to change the land." If it is living water, it brings with it the gift of reconciliation and shalom.

In the deep quiet of the canyon, I hear the sound of another river. It is every river from every continent and generation flowing into this one. Brothers and sisters, mothers and fathers, children of every color and race are gathering on its banks. We are winged dancers,

. . . .

story tellers, truth bearers, messengers of God, emissaries of the Holy Spirit, dressed in flowing white robes, moving in a dance as if one body, energy stirring from one white-robed dancer to another. Our feet miraculously move through the muddy wash of this river flowing with God's forgiveness, and we sing God's jubilant song: *"There is a river whose streams make glad the city of God, the Holy Habitation of the Most High. God is in the midst of her; she shall not be overthrown; God shall help her at the break of day."* [6]

---

6 Psalm 46: 5,6

9

Deep river, my home is over Jordan;
Deep river, I want to cross over into camp ground.
Oh, don't you want to go to that Gospel Feast,
That promise land where all is peace?
Deep river, my home is over Jordan.
Deep river, I want to cross over into camp ground.

"Paula Jean, I baptize thee in the Name of the Father, and of the Son, and of the Holy Ghost. Amen."

It is a cold, sunny Sunday morning in January of 1946 in Nashville, Tennessee. A strong, steady ray of sun cuts through the prism of the stained glass window over the baptismal font of Holy Trinity Episcopal Church, the dapples of color falling gently on the shoulders of the brown-skinned family gathered here. The large, dark man invoking these ancient words of commissioning in his deep baritone voice is my grandfather, the Rev. S.A. Morgan, priest of the Episcopal Church. He holds my two-week-old self in his large black hands, pours the living water over me, and, signing a cross on my brand new but determined forehead, he intones: *"We receive this Child into the congregation of Christ's flock; and do sign her with the sign of the Cross, in token that hereafter she shall not be ashamed to confess the faith of Christ crucified, and manfully fight under his banner, against sin, the world, and the devil; and to continue as Christ's faithful soldier and servant unto her life's end."*

I am just a baby and I have no clue what is being marked on my brow, what it is I won't be ashamed to confess, what army I am joining. But what is being marked this day by the Holy Spirit will be recalled over and over again as I learn the habit of dipping my hand in the baptismal font on the way into the assembly. With the little bit of new and yet ancient water, I make the sign of the cross on my now more weathered but still determined brow, each time refreshed anew for beginning the journey as I am sent into the world to pursue my soul's vocation. *"Let us go across to the other side."*[1] I hear a voice call to me, stirring up the waters deep within. It is a call to cross over to new beginnings, to carry on another little piece of "the work God wants done."[2]

It is late in August of 1971. Twenty-five years and fifteen hundred miles north of Nashville, my husband, John, and I are standing on the rocky cliffs of Bonaventure Island, a thousand feet above the rough, cold waters of the North Atlantic Ocean. I am seven and a half months pregnant with our first child, and we have come for one last adventure before our baby arrives. When we planned this adventure, we didn't know that life on these cliffs in late August would teach these soon-to-be parents lessons we would come to count on—lessons in faith.

Our tent has been our home for four rainy nights and days as we travel north into Quebec and east out onto the Gaspé Peninsula. We pause after each of the afternoon storms to stand on the rocky cliffs and walk in the purple-and-magenta sea of wild flowers along the narrow peninsula road. This trip was John's idea, and the cold, gray, wet weather fuels rather than dampens his naturally Nordic spirits. After almost four years of living with this person, I am still puzzled by why anyone would want to go on vacation in order to have cold feet, unruly hair, and an uncomfortably wet body. But I am slowly being won over by the monotone horizon and the fields of wild purple that the Great Gardener knew to plant

---

1 Mark 4:35

2 "Continue the work God wanted done." Joan Chittister, *Wisdom Distilled from the Daily, Living the Rule of St. Benedict Today* (San Francisco, CA.: Harper and Row, 1990)p.86μ

against this uncompetitive background. Also I have long been smitten by this man who knows to turn his back on comfort and the social niceties of life in order to gain the kind of perspective that only comes when we let the horizon work on our rough edges.

We have come all this way to see a colony of gannets, beautiful, white birds with six- and seven-foot wing spans, who raise their young at the top of the rocky cliffs of Bonaventure Island. Crossing over the rough waters from the peninsula to the island in a fisherman's vessel, we climb the steep cliffs, follow the path through the sheep meadow and the woods and out onto the high cliffs. Here we are met first by the smell and then by the sight of the gannet colony. Standing on the cliff amongst the huge, noisy, nesting parent birds, we, soon-to-be parents ourselves, have our first glimpse of what has called us to this place and time.

Late August in the colony is fledgling time, and the parent gannets are teaching their enormous babies how to fly. They lead them to the edge of the cliff, high over the cold, rocky, rough waters, and with what can only be understood as faith, they shove their babies out into the world. From what we can tell, guardian angels must do the rest of the instructing, because these awkward baby birds indeed take off, flapping their wings until they are miraculously tacking upwind and out to sea, soaring thousands of miles and years away. One day they will return to raise their own *kinder* on these cliffs, carrying on this mysterious form of apostolic succession.

It is late in August, 1993. I am on my fledgling flight as a postulant for Holy Orders, beginning my first day of seminary. My mother and I have never missed this first-day-of-school ritual, and, keeping our tradition, I have called her long distance from the downstairs pay phone of the seminary. "What are you wearing?" Mom asks. "Do have comfortable shoes?" Some things never change.

I had recently come from a week-long visit with Mom for "the treatment," as we call it —quiet, low-fat meals, clean sheets, and soaks in Mom's hot tub (healing pool, she calls it and has christened it "Siloam"). We talked and we listened. We played piano-violin and recorder-piano duets. One evening late in the visit, I told Mom that I'd been thinking that it would help me to have something of Grandfather's to carry with me (or, as my grandfather would have said, "to carry me") through seminary. "That had come to me too," Mom said.

Soon, as the sounds of my mother's rummaging through her "safe-keeping drawer" came from her bedroom, my thoughts returned to the spring before when I had traveled south to Alexandria, Virginia, as a prospective student to look over Virginia Theological Seminary. I had learned that the Bishop Payne Library there contained the archives of my grandfather's seminary, Bishop Payne Seminary, the only Episcopal divinity school for Black men of his day. I arrived at the entrance of the beautiful, pastoral campus, a brand new postulant for the priesthood, filled with curiosity and excitement about retrieving evidence of my grandfather's pilgrimage toward Holy Orders at the far end of the century. I spent the day following the little printed itinerary and map of the buildings I had been given and occasionally the lead of an enthusiastic seminarian half my age. I intentionally saved the trip to the library for a late-afternoon highlight of what I knew would be a long day.

Since the library building bore the name of my grandfather's seminary, I had been imagining that the whole building would be dedicated to the history of Black priests in the Episcopal Church. I entered the vast library space and began to search the walls for photographs of my grandfather's classmates, the ones whose stories I had so often heard him tell. I knew these men by my grandfather's great imitations of them, by the anticipated last lines of the stories he told, punctuated by his big laugh and an occasionally escaped tear wiped away with the handkerchief retrieved from his back pocket. "I like that man," he would say. "He thinks the world of me!"

· · · · · ·

After an hour or so of finding no visible evidence of the story I had come to witness, I finally decided to ask somebody where I might find the archives of the Bishop Payne Seminary. The person at the desk directed me to the basement where I soon discovered that the "archives" consisted of a few, dusty boxes of papers. Not much to show for the work of those Black men who I know, from my grandfather's stories, suffered great abuse at the hands of a system without the imagination and sense of justice to fully include their gifts. The archivist was apologetic on behalf of the seminary and, without my asking, left me alone with the small pile of boxes and my crestfallen hopes.

There must be *something* here, I thought, as I sat down and began to dig gently through this pitiful repository of memories. I was thinking, as I handled each paper with care, that the only truth these documents reveal about the lives these Black seminarians endured at the hands of the white bishops who made up the faculty and determined their fate in the church is manifested in the fragility of the paper on which they are written. Suddenly, there in my hands was the weight of one incredible treasure: the Matriculation Book of the Bishop Payne Seminary. My heart leapt in anticipation as I placed it on the table, settled at the edge of my seat, and slowly turned the old, crisp pages. There it was, signed in my grandfather's hand on Monday, September 18, 1905: "Sandy Alonzo Morgan," and then in the hand of an officer of the seminary, "graduated 1909, age 23." My eyes "filled up" as my grandfather would say about his (and they often did). The generous archivist let me carry home a photocopy to show my mother.

I was recalling this story when Mom emerged from her room with her father's gold cross and his ring in her hands. He had received the ring upon graduation from Bishop Payne Seminary. The cross is inscribed on one side with his name, "S.A. Morgan." On the other side are the dates of his ordinations to the diaconate (24 June, '09) and to the priesthood (1 December, '10). When I was growing up, I never saw Grandfather without the cross on his

· · · · · ·

chest and the ring on his hand, and it was surprising to see them, with all their familiar topography, disembodied from him now. I had always thought that Grandfather and those jewels were one and the same. And maybe they were, because when my mother put the chain that holds the ring and the cross around my neck, I had a feeling of peace.

"What are you wearing?" I hear Mom ask as I stand in the basement phone booth of the seminary. I feel the joy in her voice when I tell her that I am wearing Grandfather's cross and his seminary ring. Then, coming straight to the point of our beginning-of-school ritual, Mom asks, "How do you feel on your first day?" "Same old scary feelings," I say, "but at least they aren't *new* scary feelings." What I am feeling is echoing from every fledgling moment of every threshold of my life: *Will anybody know who I am?*

"Faith is the assurance of things hoped for, the conviction of things not seen. By faith Abraham obeyed when he was called to set out for a place that he was to receive as an inheritance, and he set out not knowing where he was going. By faith he stayed for a time in the land he had been promised, as in a foreign land, living in tents, as did Isaac and Jacob, who were heirs of the same promise....Therefore, since we are surrounded by a cloud of witnesses, let us lay aside every weight... and let us run with perseverance the race that is set before us...." [3]

I am sitting in opening chapel, hearing these words when the words become a prayer for our sojourning sons, fledgling adults out in the world. Abram Lawrence, historian, writer, and teacher, has pitched his tent half way between the western mountains and the lowlands of North Carolina, not far from the roots of his great-great-grandfather, Job Childs Lawrence, whose hard-earned name he received as an inheritance. (When he chose to go to college there, his Mississippi grandmother had remarked, "It's about time one of you-all

---

3 Hebrews 11:1-18, 12:1

in the family went south!") Our professional musician son, John Wesley, has just packed up his basses and headed across the country to the City of Angels (with his geologist father's blessing and a suggestion that he find an apartment in a building no more than three stories high). On the way, he has paused on the north rim of the Grand Canyon, five thousand feet above the Colorado River where his namesake, John Wesley Powell, the geologist who first documented the explorations of this canyon, stood a century and a quarter before. I hear the Letter to the Hebrews as a prayer that our sons will feel and hear and experience the cloud of witnesses that go beside and before them, that they will know who and whose they are as an inheritance of faith. I am reminding myself to pause in this hectic race and listen for the voices of the witnesses, including and especially our *kinder*, who with grace and strength, perseverance, and the blessings of their forebears, are running the race set before them.

I am praying for their fledgling flights (and my own), when suddenly I am remembering the way, a quarter of a century ago, the horizon gave us a glimpse of a plan God had for us bigger than the one we had for ourselves. I am remembering how the purples and magentas were planted by the Holy Spirit in the midst of my complaints about the weather. I am especially remembering the instruction in faith we were given at the top of those cliffs.

"Let us go across to the other side" calls Jesus to his disciples, and *"leaving the crowd, they took him with them in the boat, just as he was."*[4] Just as he was—worn out from teaching and healing in the small towns of Galilee, worn out from the challenges of the religious community and the pressing crowd. Just as he was—worn out enough to climb in the boat and fall fast asleep in the stern.

---

4 Mark 4:35b,36a

"Let us cross over," he had said matter-of-factly, but in his tone there had been a hint of the work that would face them on the other side where they will be strangers, radical upstarts who will surely not be welcomed in these towns. Even as they pull away from the Galilean shore, they know they are leaving well-honed careers as engineers, educators, bankers, lawyers, and doctors—to scrape out an unsure existence feeding the hungry; sheltering the poor; consoling the weak, the sick, the lonely. How will they pay for their kids' education? How will they eke out the car payments or afford health insurance? How will they manage the guilt about not visiting an aging and ailing parent a thousand or three thousand miles away? Or get to the parent conference in the middle of the school day? The very thoughts send the boat suddenly listing deep to one side and crashing waves fill the boat, and their minds and hearts too, with the murky and confusing waters.

In the stormy seas stirred up around them, I feel the ancient and current storms of transition of my own life—crossings-over from childhood to adolescence, from reasonably good health to the uncertainties of illness, from the illusion of success to the possibility of failure, from familiarity to strangeness, from connection to separation, from life to death.

"Jesus!" we call, panicking along with the seafaring disciples. "Do you not care if we perish?" We're trying to follow you, doing our best to discern a call here, and you're taking a power nap!

And now the image in my mind is a picture of myself on a stormy day in January in New York City. I am striding out of the General Theological Seminary gates into the wind and rain, in my own flesh-and-blood bad mood about being a fifty-one-year-old African-American woman living away from her husband of thirty years in a fourth-floor dormitory room built very definitely for young, single, white, nineteenth-century Anglican gentlemen. The waves of frustration coming up over me on this particular day are in the wake of the first days of an odd little hazing exercise the church calls the General Ordination Exam, in which one sits for four full days regurgitating a voiceless version of what one has supposedly digested in the way of theological training over the last three or four years. The rule is that as you write these exams you may not reveal who you are. Somehow the examiners figure that way they can be fair. They can eliminate from the ministry any "irregular people," any unworthy people, any people whose story as a child of God may be different from the story the dominant group has told itself for a couple of thousand years about who we are as a church.

The story they are examining us on is one told in unison: no women's voices, no children's voices, no voices of gays or Blacks. It is a story told in one language. It is a story that does not include the voices of the hurting people I sat with in the emergency room of a downtown hospital two summers ago. It is not a story reflecting the strength and dignity and joy of the people I worked side by side with at the St. Mary's, Chester, food cupboard. Somewhere from the distant past is the voice of a child standing at the door asking, *"Will anybody know who I am?"* But her voice will not speak up on these exams.

And so as I walk into this storm I am sailing into the faceless wind of the examiners' requirement that I be just like them, requiring of me that I recall the skill that I learned during my growing-up years in school, where I used up my intuition and creative energy adapting to a relentless string of discontinuities between who God made me on the inside and the person I needed to be on the outside in order to succeed in school. I had to unremember all over again who I was, what my story was, and become someone else in order to survive.

I have just rounded Eighteenth Street and am headed down the narrow walkway between the Westside Highway and the Hudson River. "Just exactly what did you have in mind here, God?" I am yelling my Job-like frustrations out into the fog and rain over the deserted piers. People in New York City don't seem to pay much attention when they see a grown-up lady down by the river, barking at God in the rain. They're mostly doing a bit of yelling of their own. "Do you expect me to go back and sit in that little hard chair and finish those stupid, cruel exams? And what do they have to do with my ministry anyway?"

Suddenly the waves slapping against the rotten piers seem to get higher and louder. *"Who is this that darkens counsel by words without knowledge?"*[5] demands a voice I hear out of the whirlwind. Or is that the voice of a storm now rising up inside of me? *"Where were you when I laid the foundation of the earth? Who shut in the sea with doors when it burst forth from the womb...and said 'Thus far shall you come and no farther, and here your proud waves shall be stayed.'"*[6] Who died and made you queen of the sea?

But it is a sudden clap of thunder in this winter rain storm that startles me and sends me tearing back to the refuge of the seminary close. And now, as I am running, I hear between the pounding of my feet on the wet pavement and the pounding of my heart, echoes of a deeper voice. *"She shall not be ashamed to confess the faith of Christ crucified... and fight under God's banner, against sin, the world, and the devil; and to continue as Christ's faithful soldier and servant unto her life's end."* Is it the strength of the wind at my back? Or can I really feel myself being held in my grandfather's arms, carried over the waves of frustration and exhaustion from all this rowing?

✳ ✳ ✳

Back at the seminary now, and in from the rain, I mount the four flights of stairs to my room and the next set of my waiting-to-be-finished exams. There, outside the door, is a little

---

5 Job 38:2

6 Job 38:4,8,11

brown bag, stuffed full of cards and letters of encouragement. They are love messages from the very people whose voices I had thought were absent. I sit down on my dormitory floor in a wet pool of my own weariness and read the messages slowly.

"Hang in there," says one voice. I can see her vibrant face sitting in the pew, hanging in there with her own little flock. "You have the special strength and goodness for this work. We miss your light." "If anyone can pass 'em, you can," says the voice of one who has been my teacher through it all. "From the place of wilderness comes truth and beauty and the knowledge of self in the name of the Spirit," says a voice I recognize by its own truth and beauty and self-knowledge. "This wilderness will be traveled through soon," she writes. "Your guardian angel will be with you," says one who has definitely been my guardian angel. "You've always helped me. God bless you." "Remember that the Lord holds your hand and walks this road with you, immersing you in his wisdom and strength," writes one whose light I can feel as I read her words. "It's okay to be afraid," says one voice familiar from my childhood.

And then, a voice that draws me all the way out of my somewhat self-inflicted storminess into a burst of joyous laughter—right up here all by myself in my little room. It is the voice of a young man, strong and clear as it is when he greets me at the Peace on an ordinary Sunday. "PAULA," he writes in big determined letters that sum up all of the caring that has been heaped on him in love through his life, and all the love I've had heaped on me from the generations before me, beside me, and now the ones that follow. His message sums up the love heaped on all creation by the Everliving, Everloving One who laid the foundation of the earth and *"made the clouds its garment, then lovingly swaddled all of creation in a soothing band of darkness and hung the morning stars."* [7]

---

7 Job 38:9

"PAULA, DO YOUR BEST—DON'T QUIT—AMEN." I hear in his words the love of God carried to him by all those who told him to do his best and who never quit on him. I feel in his words the calm the disciples must have felt when Jesus rose up in that storm-rocked boat and demanded of the wind: *"Peace! Be still!"*[8]

Peace, be still, he says into the tempests of my life as I cross over to do the work God gives us to do. And in that word of peace, I know who I am and whose I am, and I take up the oars and begin to cross over. I hear in the now-gathered voices the refrain of the psalmist's song: *"Then were they glad because of the calm, and God brought them to the harbor they were bound for."*[9]

---

8 Mark 4:39

9 Psalm 107, vs. 30 (translation from *Psalter for the Christian People* edited by Gordon Lathrop and Gail Ramshaw. Collegeville, MN.: Liturgical Press, 1993, p.149)

Epilogue

"The kingdom of heaven is like yeast that a woman took and mixed in with three measures of flour until all of it was leavened."[1]

On a clear, crisp mid-September day in 1976, I am baking bread at the kitchen counter when the phone rings. It is my parents calling from the midst of the whirlwind of the Episcopal Church's General Convention in Minneapolis. My father, chairman of the Committee on the Ordination of Women to the Priesthood and Episcopate, has kept me abreast of progress on the resolution to open the historic, apostolic Episcopal priesthood and episcopacy to women, and I know it is due to come before the House for a final vote.

History had already been made the day before when the House of Deputies of the Convention unanimously elected as its President, Charles Lawrence, the first Black person ever to be elected to lead the 187-year old legislative body. The convention paper had reported, "The House of Deputies gave a standing ovation to Dr. Charles R. Lawrence and again to his wife, Dr. Margaret Morgan Lawrence, after his election." From our homes in Boston and San Francisco and Philadelphia, Margaret and Charles' three grown children participated in that standing ovation, knowing the gentleness and courage, the passion, patience, fairness, wisdom and levity Dad would bring to this new phase of his work. We also knew from our vantage point as his children, that he would make it look easier than we all knew it was and when praised and honored, would simply say as he always had, "I am blessed."

"P. Jean, it's your Pa," says Dad when I answer the phone. "Turn on the TV news," and the triumph and joy and tears I hear in his voice make me know something wonderful has

---

1 Matthew 13:33

. . . . . .

113

happened. My hands, covered with bread-dough mess, put down the phone, reach for the TV switch and struggle to adjust the broken antennae just in time to see a clip of the Convention floor crowded with relieved, resigned, and jubilant deputies. There, in the midst of them, is my mother, priest's daughter from Mississippi, radiant, joyful, and as beautiful as I've ever seen her! I pick up the receiver again. My dad has given the phone to my mom on the other end. "Thanks be to God!" she says through tears of her own.

I put the phone down, turn off the television and resume my bread baking. As my hands find their way back to the familiar rhythms of this weekly ritual, I see my grandmother's hands baking the cake from scratch with the touch of an angel. "So light it wouldn't hurt a flea," was the highest praise she would give her own results. I see my mother's hands confidently "cutting" the biscuit dough. "Maggie, you have outdone yourself!" my father never failed to say as he savored the freshly buttered golden brown fruits of her labor of love. I see in my hands seasons and years of orchestrating the little hands of kindergarten children as they mixed and kneaded, punched and pulled the dough. I see the hands of my own children, who learned to make the weekly bread with me, standing on stools at this kitchen counter. "*Mama's little baby loves shortnin', shortnin', Mama's little baby loves shortnin' bread,*" we sang as they squeezed and pushed the dough to their heart's content. It was "challah bread" we were making, though they forever called it "Paula bread" and insisted that we make a "love loaf" for the family to eat as soon as it came out of the oven. They knew too well my inclination to give bread away.

I am thinking of about this inclination as I fold the bread over one last time before covering it and setting it aside to rise, when my thoughts return to the vote for women's ordination. Maybe some day I will make a little love loaf to bless and give away. Maybe the inclination to give the bread away is who I am.

· · · · · ·

✱ ✱ ✱

"Jesus said to her, 'Mary!' She turned and said to him in Hebrew, "Rabbouni!" (which means Teacher)."[2]

It is the Feast of Mary and Martha 1999, the twenty-fifth anniversary of the ordinations of the first women priests. We have gathered at the Church of the Advocate, the site of the historic ordinations of the "Philadelphia Eleven," to celebrate and give thanks for these women whose vocations called them to minister to the church ahead of its own time. Bishop Robert DeWitt had written, "It is ironic that what happened 25 years ago here at the Advocate was for a time seen more as an issue of three misbehaving bishops, than as a breakthrough created by eleven pioneering women. Make no mistake, the event was a creative action of, by and for women. The bishops were only accessories. The 'Philadelphia Eleven' belong with the likes of Susan B. Anthony and Rosa Parks. They are of that goodly company of women through history who have seen that in overcoming the restrictions which circumscribed their own lives they brought release to countless others."

When asked by the "sisters" to be the celebrant for the Eucharist, I hesitated for only a moment. In that moment I heard my father's voice repeating what he'd said to me twenty years before when, as President of the House, he called to invite me to serve on the Standing Liturgical Commission. "I'm not going to twist your arm," he said, "but I'm not going to take 'no' for an answer." Then he said something else I'd heard before: "Know that I am with you."

And so, as we gather on this great day, he is here in the stories of the women and men who meet me and realize that I am Charles Lawrence's daughter. "Your father was so gracious," says one woman priest. "He blessed us on our journey," another tells me. "Dr.

---

2 John 20:16

Lawrence sought me out and called me by my name," says a woman bishop who is known by her flock as one who seeks out others, calling them by their names. My mother has been invited to process in "The Church of Hope" procession. As the service begins with the fiercely hopeful rhythms of African drums, I look out from the side aisle where my sister deacon and I are waiting, and I see Dr. Margaret Lawrence arm in arm with our dear friend and brother priest. His long stride is equal to two or three of her steps as she literally dances up the aisle.

"Send your Holy Spirit upon us and upon these gifts of bread and wine that they may be to us the Body and Blood of your Christ. Grant that we, burning with your Spirit's power, may be a people of hope, justice, and love." The words of blessing come through me from a place at once deep and broad and near. This moment is every moment my hands have ever held the bread, mixing in the leavening, kneading, setting it aside to rise. And then in the breaking, it is every moment I have ever had the inclination to feed hungry mouths, to give the bread away.

"The Bread of Heaven," I say, looking into the bright, engaging eyes of a beautiful, young woman standing before me with outstretched hands. I break off a little piece of the bread and put it into her hands. When she has eaten it, she says, "Thank you, Teacher Paula." "Teacher," I hear, *"Rabbouni."* And then I see who she is. She is one of my kindergarten children from years ago, one whose hands had helped to mix the leavening into the bread. "You are welcome, Carrie," I say. And then as I turn to the next pair of open hands, I hear the answer to the prayer that has fueled my lifetime of seeking to open doors so that every child will be free to come home to the gift of God within. *Yes, they will know who I am. Yes, we know who and whose we are by the gathering of our gifts.*

. . . . . .